P9-BXZ-906

COMPUTER
ACCOUNTING
METHODS

COMPUTER ACCOUNTING METHODS

featuring

BASIC Programming on a Time-sharing Computer

GREGORY A. COOK
UNIVERSITY OF DENVER

BARBARA J. WADE
THE SERVICE BUREAU COMPANY

CLARK C. UPTON
THE SERVICE BUREAU COMPANY

FIRST EDITION

petrocelli books, NEW YORK 1974

Copyright © Mason & Lipscomb Publishers, Inc. 1975

Published simultaneously in the United Kingdom by Mason & Lipscomb
Publishers, Inc., London, England.

All rights reserved. No part of this work covered by the copyrights hereon may
be reproduced or used in any form or by any means—graphic, electronic, or
mechanical, including photocopying, recording, or taping, or information
storage and retrieval systems—without written permission of the publisher.

First Printing

Printed in the United States of America

Library of Congress Cataloging in Publication Data

Cook, Gregory A   1950-
    Computer accounting methods, featuring BASIC program-
ming on a time-sharing computer.

    Includes index.
    1. Electronic data processing--Accounting. 2. Basic
(Computer program language) 3. Time-sharing computer
systems.   I. Wade, Barbara J., 1942-   joint author.
II. Upton, Clark C., joint author.   III. Title.
HF5657.C66 1974   657'.028'54   74-23664
ISBN 0-88405-293-1

CONTENTS

PREFACE

Business transaction recording and bookkeeping are performed to provide an accounting of the operating results and the status of a business. Data processing is a mechanized procedure of organizing the data into meaningful results. Computerized accounting is a form of data processing. It has made up-to-the-minute accounting possible for today's high volume of business transactions.

Although there are many different computerized accounting systems, some fundamental methods are common to most systems. To illustrate these methods, several of the classic accounting systems will be used as examples in this book. Many business managers will have programmers or even automatic report-generation systems available to them; however, these conditions do not eliminate the need to understand data processing concepts.

The presentations of General Ledger, Accounts Receivable, and Payroll on a computer time-sharing system are not meant to be a general recommendation that businesses should perform these functions on a time-sharing system. The time-sharing computer and the BASIC programming language have been used to provide a simplicity that will minimize discussion of the technical aspects of the computer. The reader is then able to concentrate on the specific accounting problem and the data processing concepts inherent in it.

1

INTRODUCTION TO DATA PROCESSING SYSTEMS

Accounting information is essential to the functioning of any business. Only by having reliable and accurate financial information can the businessman maintain control of his organization.

THE NEED FOR COMPUTERIZED ACCOUNTING INFORMATION

To survive in today's competitive environment, the businessman must have financial information that is:

1. Timely; that is, current.
2. Accurate.
3. Easily accessible.
4. In the right form for use.

A well-conceived and well-run automated accounting system provides information that best meets these requirements. The explosion of financial data has brought organizational managers to recognize that only a computerized system can produce results which meet all four criteria. The basic reason is that the speed and accuracy of a computer provides rapid classification and manipulation of large volumes of data. And so the accountant must have basic knowledge of computer accounting methods as well as of accounting theory and practice. With this combined understanding, he has a basis to utilize computer systems effectively in order to produce meaningful and timely financial information.

PURPOSE OF THE BOOK

This book is designed to provide the computer concepts and techniques needed for accounting purposes. The mechanical and electronic components of the computer will be discussed only insofar as they affect the design of a computerized accounting system. The approach emphasizes present methods of adapting accounting functions to computers and includes (1) a review of computer fundamentals; (2) a discussion of systems design; and (3) examples of accounting programs on a time-shared computer. A time-shared computer simultaneously serves many users from remote terminals. It is accessible to most colleges and universities as well as the business community.

A review of the fundamental requirements for automated accounting information systems must begin with an examination of the basic elements of a data processing system. The processing system may be manual, partly automated, or fully computerized. Common to most data processing systems are:

1. Permanent Memory—a permanent storage area for procedures and information when not in use.
2. Working Memory—a storage area for procedures and information while being processed or updated.
3. Processing Unit—the controller of the processing, mathematical calculations, and logical decisions.

THE MANUAL SYSTEM

In a manual system, the permanent memory may be ledger pages, the working memory a scratch pad, and the processing unit a combination of human brain power and an adding machine. The primary limitations of a manual system are (1) that information from permanent memory must be read and manually entered, and (2) that human errors occur in the processing procedure. Speed and accuracy conflict in the manual system.

MACHINE ACCOUNTING SYSTEMS

Bookkeeping machines help decrease human errors and give speed to the processing procedure. The many types of bookkeeping machines vary from simple adding machines to modern electronic computers. However, only by means of the computer can a system be fully automated.

The central processing unit (CPU) controls the computer system. This text assumes that the computer has a large permanent memory (on-line storage) connected directly to the processing unit, to allow rapid movement of information to and from working memory. In this computer system, the permanent memory stores accounting records, the working memory stores the processing instructions, and the processing unit does the calculations and processing of the data for reports and permanent records. Permanent records are stored in groups, called "data files," in permanent memory.

It is important for the reader to realize that this text does not discuss all aspects of using the time-sharing computer. The material covered is deemed essential for accounting and does not include some system features, programming statements, and additional types of terminals that may be used in some accounting systems.

USING THE COMPUTER

Time sharing is a form of data processing that permits many users to have simultaneous access to a computer system. Usually, the computer is fast enough so that each user perceives that he is getting the "full attention" of the computer. Communication with the computer is accomplished by a keyboard printer device called a "communications terminal," which is often a Teletype.* Users are connected to the computer through regular telephone lines by dialing a special telephone number. When the connection is made, a sign-on message is printed on the user's terminal, asking for his user number and password. After signing on correctly, the user has access to the capabilities of the computer.

Simplicity of use is the key ingredient in the fast-growing popularity of computer time-sharing systems. The absence of any "middleman" allows access to the computer at the convenience of the user. He may use some predefined procedures (programs) that are already stored in the computer, or he can develop his own programs, using the BASIC programming language. Each user is assigned a portion of permanent memory where he can save his predefined procedures (programs) and information (data files).

A collection of similar information stored on the computer is called a "data file." There are two types of data files: source and binary.

Source data files can be created directly by typing in the data on the terminal keyboard; *binary* files must be created as output of a program. Each has benefits and limitations. Source data files are convenient for entering data and are easy to print (list) on the terminal. Binary data files are stored in the "machine language" of the computer and are processed more efficiently than source data because no translation is necessary.

A computerized accounting system has two main classes of data files: master files and transaction files. A master file is a permanent file, probably containing a record of each account and its current balance. In addition to keeping the account balances up to date, the accounting system must provide for adding of new records and deleting records from the file. The binary type of data file is normally used for accounting master files. A transaction file is a collection of records describing specific business transactions including the dollar amount of the transaction. These records are normally retained for the one accounting period in which they are posted (added) to the account balances in the appropriate master file records.

Since source data files are convenient to enter into the computer and easy to print on the terminal for verification, the source type is often used for transaction files. The words "data" and "master" are often implied (not stated) in referring to data files. The General Ledger file means the General Ledger master data file and the transaction file means the transaction data file.

---

*Trademark of the Teletype Corporation, Skokie, Illinois.

System Commands

System commands are simple words representative of actions to be performed. Only by means of commands can a user initiate action by the computer. The commands to be discussed are:

CLEAR	RUN
NAME	CATALOG
SAVE	PURGE
LOAD	FILE
LIST	OFF

Commands differ from program statements. A program statement begins with a line number, to determine its position within the program, and is executed in turn only after the user has issued the RUN command. A command is not preceded by a line number and is executed immediately. The commands listed above are defined as follows:

CLEAR   This command is used to clear the user's working memory of any program or source data file; it erases anything there, including a name. The CLEAR command has no effect on permanent memory.

NAME   This command is used to assign a name to a program or source data file in working memory. The command must be followed by the name to be assigned. Any previously assigned name is changed to the new one. A program may be RUN without a name, but it cannot be SAVEd.

SAVE   This command places a copy of the contents of the user's working memory into permanent memory with its assigned name. A name is required before the working memory can be SAVEd because the name is the means of locating the program or data file in permanent memory.

LOAD   This command must be followed by a name. The LOAD command (e.g., LOAD PROGRAM1) first CLEARs working memory and then moves a *copy* of the specified program or source data file in permanent memory *to working memory.*

LIST   This command causes the sequential line-by-line printing of the contents of working memory. As previously stated, programs and source data files are entered, using line numbers that determine the sequential order of the lines.

RUN   This command causes the execution of the program statements in working memory. The actual sequence is to translate (compile) the program statements into "machine language" instructions and then execute these instructions. If the command is followed by a name, then a LOAD is performed before the RUN. For example, RUN PROGRAM 1 is an example of a normal command to RUN a program named PROGRAM 1 that has not previously been LOADed.

CATALOG   This command is used to print the names of all programs and data files stored in the user's permanent memory. This is important to review frequently because most systems charge a fee for the amount of permanent memory used. Obsolete or worthless programs should be removed.

PURGE   This command must be followed by a name. It is used to remove (erase) the specified program or data file from permanent memory. It has no effect on working memory.

FILE   This command must be followed by a name. It allocates space for a *binary* data file with the specified name. It does not put data in the file, but only initializes the file; presumably, a program will later put in the data.

OFF   This command is used to disconnect the user from the computer time-sharing system. It causes the system to print a sign-off message on the user's terminal and then break the connection with the terminal.

The following pages show an example of a sequence of actions performed by a time-sharing system user.

The user dials the telephone number of the time-sharing system and receives the sign-on message. He types in his user number and password.

He types in a seven-line program.

He assigns a name (PROG4) to the program.

He lists out the program to verify that it has been entered correctly.

He sees an error in line 160 and corrects it by retyping the line.

Now that the program is correct, he will SAVE it in permanent memory.

Now he RUNs the program to determine that it works properly.

Next he may CLEAR his working memory because he is thinking of entering a second program.

```
                    USER NUMBER,PASSWORD--
                    ████░░█░█░░░░░░░░░░█░██░░░░░░░░░░░░░░░░░░
                              (computer overprints entry)
                              (... to retain security   )


                    100 PRINT 'ENTER TWO VALUES TO BE ADDED ';
(user enters)       110 INPUT X, Y
(these seven)       120 IF X = 0 GOTO 170
(lines      )       130 LET Z = X + Y
                    140 PRINT Z
                    160 GOTO 105
                    170 END


                    NAME PROG4
                    READY

                    LIST

                    PROG4

                    100 PRINT 'ENTER TWO VALUES TO BE ADDED ';
                    110 INPUT X, Y
                    120 IF X = 0 GOTO 170
                    130 LET Z = X + Y
                    140 PRINT Z
                    160 GOTO 105
                    170 END


                    160 GOTO 100


                    SAVE
                    READY


                    RUN

                    PROG4

                    ENTER TWO VALUES TO BE ADDED ? 23, 54
                     77
                    ENTER TWO VALUES TO BE ADDED ? 44, 3.6
                     47.6
                    ENTER TWO VALUES TO BE ADDED ? 0, 0

                    PROCESSING      0 UNITS


                    CLEAR
                    READY


                         Note: an underline indicates a user entry
```

Before continuing, he checks what he has now stored in permanent memory.

After noting that a worthless demonstration program (DEMO) is still stored, he decides to PURGE it.

He enters CATALOG again to verify that DEMO is really removed.

He now plans to use a prewritten program supplied by the time-sharing service. This program requires a binary file in which the program will place the resulting data for further use. This binary data file must be initialized.

Suddenly an associate tells him of a project that must take priority over this work. Therefore, he will sign off the system and continue his computer project at a later time.

```
CATALOG

DEMO      PROG1      PROG3      PROG4


PURGE DEMO
READY

CATALOG

PROG1      PROG3      PROG4




FILE STATDATA
READY




OFF
SIGNING OFF AT 10:38
CONNECT TIME 11 MINUTES
PROCESSING     0 UNITS
```

Note: an underline indicates a user entry

QUESTIONS

1. Where are procedures or information stored when not in use?
2. What is one limitation of a manual accounting system?
3. What types of data files are processed more efficiently by the computer? Why?
4. What does the NAME command do?
5. Do records in a transaction file usually contain account balances?
6. The SAVE command requires that a name must be assigned to the contents of working memory before the command can be executed.
   True _____ False _____?
7. What is the use of the CATALOG command?
8. How do you correct an error in a program statement?

2

FLOWCHARTS

Basic Learning Objective: To understand the use of flowcharts.
Specific Objectives
1. To understand the function of system flowcharts.
2. To understand the function of program flowcharts.
3. To understand the meaning of symbols, flowlines, and arrowheads.

FLOWCHARTING TECHNIQUES

A complex accounting system is difficult to design or understand without documentation. Because of this, flowcharts are used as aids to illustrate the logic and operations involved in an accounting process. Flowcharts contain symbols, flowlines, and arrowheads. The flowlines and arrowheads represent the sequence of processing. The different symbols represent different types of actions.

Flowcharts may be classified into two categories: (1) system flowcharts and (2) program flowcharts. The following sections describe the characteristics of these two types of flowcharts.

System Flowcharts

System flowcharts describe general processes such as an Accounts Receivable, Accounts Payable, or Payroll accounting system. Figure 2.1 illustrates and explains the various system flowcharting symbols and their descriptions. System flowcharts describe a manual, mechanical, or a computerized process. A complete system flowchart (1) describes the operations of one or more computer programs within an accounting system, (2) indicates the sequential running order of the system, (3) indicates the data files required and produced by each program, and (4) shows documents produced by each program within the accounting system. Figure 2.2 illustrates a system flowchart for a hotel reservation system. This system is designed to illustrate the function of flowcharts in a business system. In reality, however, the system for hotel reservations would be more complex.

Symbol	*Represents*
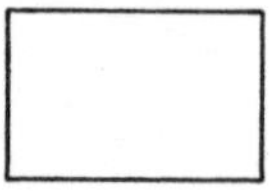	*Processing*—A major processing function (i.e., running of a program).
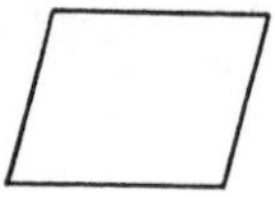	*Input/Output*—Any type of medium or data entered into or produced by a system.
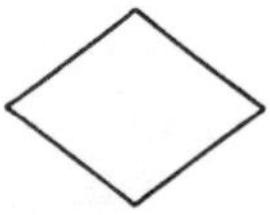	*Decision*—The decision function is used to document points in the system where a branch to alternate paths is possible, based upon variable conditions.
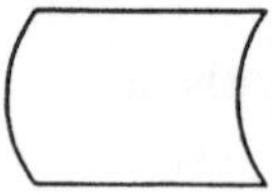	*On-Line Data File*—This symbol indicates a data file in permanent memory, connected directly to the central processing unit.
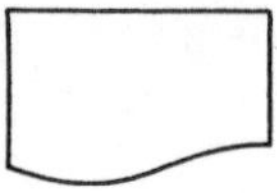	*Document*—Paper documents and reports of all varieties.
	*Connector*—Used to indicate entry from, or exist to, another part of the system flowchart.
	*Page Connector*—Used to indicate entry from, or exit to, another page in the flowchart.
	Terminal—The terminal symbol indicates a beginning or ending point in the flowchart.
	*Arrowheads and Flowlines*—Arrowhead and flowline symbols show operations sequence and data flow direction.

Fig. 2.1 System flowcharting symbols and their descriptions.

Represents	*Flowchart*

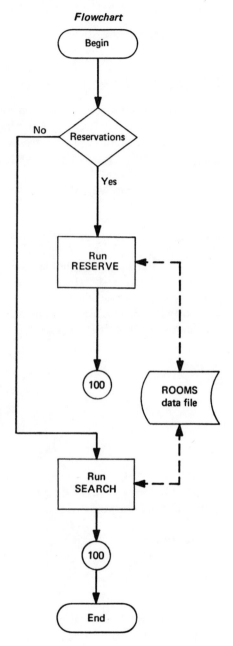

The BEGIN symbol indicates the starting point of the reservation system.

The decision symbol questions whether the customer has reservations. The symbol branches to the RESERVE program on a positive response and to the SEARCH program on a negative response.

The RESERVE program searches the data file called ROOMS for the customer's name. If the customer's name is located, the RESERVE program will print out the reserved room number.

The ROOMS data file contains the names and assigned room numbers of all customers who have reservations.

The SEARCH program is run if the customer does not have reservations. It is designed to search the ROOMS data file and locate and assign a room number to the customer.

The connector symbol indicates entry from the other branch of the system.

The terminal symbol indicates the end of the reservation system.

Fig. 2.2 System flowchart (for hotel reservations).

Uses of Symbols for Systems Flowcharting

Processing Symbol

In systems flowcharting the processing indicates any major processing function. Often it indicates the running of a particular computer program. In the hotel reservations example, the processing symbol is used to indicate the running of the programs: RESERVE and SEARCH.

Input/Output Symbol

The input/output symbol in a system flowchart indicates information available for processing (input) or recording of processed information (output). This symbol is especially useful where specification of medium is neither important nor desirable. A simple manual payroll accounting system would require three flowcharting symbols.

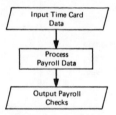

This three-step system flowchart indicates that (1) the time cards are used as input into the system, (2) the payroll data is processed, and (3) payroll checks are produced (output)

Decision

The decision symbol is used to document points in a system where a branch to alternative paths is possible, based on variable conditions. Figuratively, the symbol represents a switch.

In the reservations system flowchart it represents a two-sided switch.

The symbol questions if the customer has reservations. If the answer is "yes," control continues on the "yes" path; if the answer is "no," control continues on the "no" path.

On-Line Storage Symbol

The on-line storage symbol indicates a data file in permanent memory, one that is directly accessible to the central processing unit. This type of permanent memory is often called "direct access" or "on-line" storage. The ROOMS file in the reservations system is a data file containing the names and assigned room numbers of all customers who have reservations. The ROOMS file is connected to the RESERVE and SEARCH programs by dotted lines, indicating that both programs access the ROOMS data file.

Document

The document symbol represents paper documents and reports of all varieties. Payroll registers, general journals, and Trial Balances are all examples of documents.

Connector Symbol

Connectors are used to indicate entry from, or exit to, another part of the system flowchart. A set of two or more connector symbols with the same number are used to represent a continued flow when the use of a line is precluded by the physical or esthetic limitations of the flowchart.

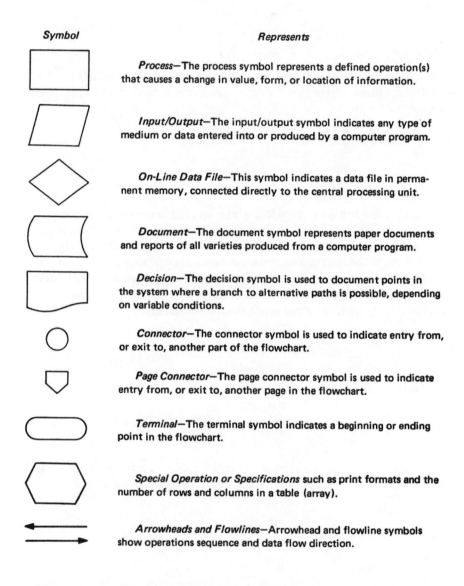

Symbol	Represents

Process—The process symbol represents a defined operation(s) that causes a change in value, form, or location of information.

Input/Output—The input/output symbol indicates any type of medium or data entered into or produced by a computer program.

On-Line Data File—This symbol indicates a data file in permanent memory, connected directly to the central processing unit.

Document—The document symbol represents paper documents and reports of all varieties produced from a computer program.

Decision—The decision symbol is used to document points in the system where a branch to alternative paths is possible, depending on variable conditions.

Connector—The connector symbol is used to indicate entry from, or exit to, another part of the flowchart.

Page Connector—The page connector symbol is used to indicate entry from, or exit to, another page in the flowchart.

Terminal—The terminal symbol indicates a beginning or ending point in the flowchart.

Special Operation or Specifications such as print formats and the number of rows and columns in a table (array).

Arrowheads and Flowlines—Arrowhead and flowline symbols show operations sequence and data flow direction.

Fig. 2.3 Program flowcharting symbols.

16

Page Connector Symbol

The page connector symbol indicates entry from, or exit to, another page in the flowchart.

PROGRAM FLOWCHARTS

A program flowchart is a blueprint of a computer program. In other words, a program flowchart indicates the operations, decisions, and the flow of processing in a program. It is detailed and specific, and usually is closely correlated with the program statements. Figure 2.3 illustrates the various program flowcharting symbols and their descriptions.

A program flowchart serves two functions: (1) It provides the fundamental guidelines for writing a computer program, and (2) it serves as a document for future reference if the program ever needs to be altered.

Figure 2.4 shows a program flowchart for the RESERVE program in the hotel reservations system.

As you can see, the flow of processing follows the direction of the arrowheads in the flowchart. Generally, the flow runs from top to bottom and from left to right.

Uses of Symbols for Program Flowcharting

Processing Symbol

This symbol orders any processing function such as defined operation(s) that cause change in value, form, or location of information. Arithmetic instructions and arithmetic assignment statements are placed in the symbol. For example, the calculation of the total cost of a product (selling price plus sales tax), is represented by:

COST = PRICE + TAX

Input/Output

Flowchart	Explanation
Begin	The BEGIN symbol indicates the starting point of the program.
Enter name	The input/output symbol indicates that the customer's name is entered by the reservations clerk into the terminal.
GET next reservation record	The input/output symbol indicates that a record containing a name and reserved room number is read from a data file (ROOMS).
Match ? — Yes → (100)	The decision symbol indicates that the program tests to see if the customer's name entered from the terminal *matches* the name read from the ROOMS data file.
Last record ?	The next decision symbol indicates that control is transferred back to GET another record if the last record has not been read.
Print no reservations under this name	If all records in the ROOMS data file have been read, and the customer's name is not matched with one of them, then the program instructs the computer to print out NO RESERVATIONS UNDER THIS NAME.
(200)	
(100)	The page connector symbol indicates the start of the second page of the program flowchart; also an entry point.
Print reserved room no.	The input/output symbol indicates that the reserved room number would be printed.
(200)	The connector symbol indicates that the program can be entered at this point from another part of the program.
End	The terminal symbol indicates the end of the program.

Fig. 2.4 Program flowchart for the RESERVE program.

18

The input/output symbol indicates that the program requires or produces some type of information. In time-sharing systems, the information may be input from, or output to, the terminal or a data file in permanent memory.

Decision Symbol

The decision symbol indicates a decision or switching type of operation that determines which of a number of alternative paths should be followed. A decision symbol generally indicates a comparison between two values, either numeric or alphabetic. For example:

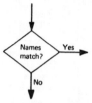

EXAMPLE. Computing State Sales Tax. Most states in the United States levy some type of sales tax. In this example, the state requires a sales tax on all salable goods except food. This sales tax is collected quarterly by the state. Instructions for computing state sales tax are as follows:

1. Total receipts must be reported in every tax return, including all sales and all services, both taxable and nontaxable.
2. Sales of nontaxable merchandise may be deducted from total receipts.
3. Net taxable sales are taxed at a rate of 4%.
4. Goods that have been purchased tax free and taken from stock for personal or business use are subject to a 3% use tax.

A program flowchart for computing state sales tax is shown in Fig. 2.5.

SUMMARY

System and program flowcharts are essential tools for the development and maintenance of accounting systems and programs. System flowcharts describe complete accounting systems, and program flowcharts illustrate the characteristics of an individual computer program. It is essential to understand the fundamentals of flowcharts because the primary structure of an accounting system is a series of logical steps, and the best means of illustrating these steps is a flowchart.

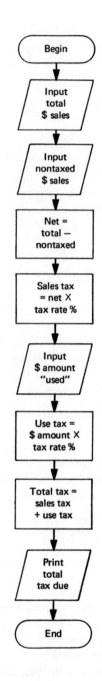

Fig. 2.5 Program flowchart for computing taxes due.

QUESTIONS

1. What is the difference between a system flowchart and a program flow-chart?
2. What is the function of a system flowchart?
3. What is the function of a program flowchart?
4. What is the function of a decision symbol in a system flowchart?
5. What type of symbol would you use to represent a payroll register in a system flowchart?
6. What symbol would you use to represent the running of a particular pro-gram in a system flowchart?
7. In the system flowchart for the hotel reservations system (Fig. 2.2), could you replace the connector symbol with a connecting line? Why?

PROBLEMS

1. Draw a program flowchart to illustrate the following routine:
   (a) Begin.
   (b) Input a value from a remote terminal and assign it to a variable named A.
   (c) Input another value from the remote terminal and assign it to a variable named B.
   (d) Perform the following process: F=(1.5*A) / (16+B).
   (e) Print out the values for A, B, and C.
   (f) End.

2. McGreggor tax service has developed a two-program system to compute personal income tax. If a client wants to create a short-form income tax state-ment that uses the standard deduction, he runs the program named SHORT. Otherwise, the client would run a program named LONG, which allows all deductions. *Required:* You are to draw an operational system flowchart that would illustrate McGreggor's system.

3. The SEARCH program in the operational system flowchart for the hotel reservation system (Fig. 2.2) is used to locate an unreserved room for a cus-tomer. This program functions as follows:
   (a) Begin.
   (b) The customer's name is input from a remote terminal and assigned to the variable called C$.
   (c) The variables N$ and R are read from the ROOMS storage file.
   (d) If N$ equals six blank spaces, then R$ is equal to C$, N$ and R are printed on the ROOMS file and on the remote terminal, and the program ends.

(e) If N$ equals any name—i.e., anything except the six blank spaces—
     the computer is instructed to read another name and room num-
     ber LN$ and R from the ROOMS storage file. *Required:* You are
     to draw a systems flowchart to illustrate this program.

3

THE BASIC PROGRAMMING LANGUAGE

General Learning Objective: To understand a program written in the BASIC programming language.

Specific Objectives

1. To understand the action performed by the BASIC statements presented.
1. To be able to read and follow the logic and flow of a BASIC program.

PROGRAMMING IN BASIC

In the computer, the central processing unit (CPU) receives its instructions from a program in working memory. A program is a series of logical steps to perform a defined procedure. These steps are expressed in statements, one to a line. All programs in this book are written in the BASIC programming language. This language was developed for, and is the most universally accepted as, the programming language for time-sharing computer systems. It is easy to understand and use. We may therefore discuss computerized accounting methods with minimal involvement with the technicalities of the computer.

The main types of statements in a computer program are listed in Table 3.1. Figure 3.1 presents programs written in BASIC.

In BASIC programs, each statement must have a line number that will determine the processing order of the statements. Programs will be stored in permanent memory with a unique name.

Note in the third example program in Fig. 3.1 that the "file" statements (150, 170, 210, 230) have a number after the OPEN, GET, or PUT. This is called a "port" (or device) number. The OPEN statement specifies the port number as well as the use of the file for input or output. This method provides for a GET or PUT statement to access the proper file by use of the appropriate port number followed by a colon and then the variable names for the data.

23

Table 3.1   Program Statements

Type	BASIC Statement	Action
Input	INPUT	Requests data be entered from the terminal (keyboard) during the processing of the program.
	GET	Reads data previously stored in a data file in permanent memory.
Output	PRINT	Prints information on the terminal printer. PRINT USING 210 means that line 210 specifies the format of the printing.
	PUT	Writes data to a data file in permanent memory.
Processing	LET	Assigns a value to a variable.
	GOTO	Control always branches to the specified statement.
	IF	Control goes to the specified statement only if the stated condition is met; otherwise, control passes to the statement on the next line.
Other statements	OPEN	Attach a data file to a program for either input or output (not both).
	DIM	Specifies the dimensions of an array (defines the number of rows and columns in a list or a table).
	REMARK	A remark by the programmer to explain program statements. It does not perform any action.
	: ###.##	Image statement. Specifies the format of printing. At left is only one of numerous possible print formats. The contents of a variable or constant specified in a PRINT USING statement will be printed just as the # signs are arranged. Other characters in the image statement will be printed as they appear.
	END	Indicates the end of the program and causes the processing to stop when this statement is executed.

```
100 INPUT X, Y
120 LET Z = X + Y
130 PRINT Z
140 END
```

```
100 PRINT 'ENTER TWO VALUES TO BE ADDED ';
110 INPUT X, Y
120 IF X = 0 GOTO 170
130 LET Z = X + Y
140 PRINT Z
160 GOTO 100
170 END
```

```
100 REMARK:   THIS PROGRAM WILL GET 10 VALUES FROM
110 REMARK    A DATA FILE, PLACE THEM IN AN ARRAY,    (an array is a list)
120 REMARK    AND THEN PRINT & PUT THEM IN ANOTHER    (or table of values)
130 REMARK    DATA FILE.
140 DIM A(10)
150 OPEN 1, 'STATFILE', INPUT
160 LET C = C + 1
170 GET   1:  A(C)
180 IF C <> 10 GOTO 160
190 REMARK:   NOW, IN REVERSE ORDER, PRINT AND PUT
200 REMARK    THE VALUES IN THE NEW DATA FILE.
210 OPEN 2, 'NEWFILE', OUTPUT
220 PRINT USING 240, A(C)
230 PUT   2:  A(C)
240 : ###.##
250 LET C = C - 1
260 IF C <> 0 GOTO 220
270 END
```

Fig. 3.1 Examples of programs written in BASIC.

   Calculations are performed in a manner similar to algebraic operations. Arithmetic operations on the right side of an equal (=) sign are called an "expression" (e.g., LET X = Y + 4).

   Arithmetic signs (operators) must be explicitly stated (not implied) in all expressions (e.g., X * Y is proper; XY is improper).

   The arithmetic operations are:

+	addition
−	subtraction
*	multiplication
/	division
↑ }	raised to the power of
** }	(both symbols are acceptable)

   The computer processes an expression based upon a hierarchy of arithmetic operators. That hierarchy is:

↑	first level
* or /	second level
+ or −	third level

Calculations of the same level are performed in the order in which they appear from left to right.

   The following list illustrates the steps the computer would use to solve the formula X = 10 ↑ 2 + 3 * 4 / 2:

Step 1.	10 ↑ 2 = 100	first level of hierarchy
Step 2.	3 * 4 = 12	second level, first from left to right
Step 3.	12 / 2 = 6	second level
Step 4.	100 + 6 = 106	third level
Step 5.	X = 106	assign the value calculated to the variable X

Parentheses cause overriding the normal order (do the calculations within parentheses first). The computer would solve the formula X = 10 ↑ (2 + 3) * 4 by the following steps:

Step 1.	(2 + 3) = 5	highest level
Step 2.	10 ↑ 5 = 100000	second level
Step 3.	100000 * 4 = 400000	third level
Step 4.	X = 400000	assign the value calculated to the variable X

Relational operators are used in the IF statement to test the comparative magnitude of two values. These operators are:

< less than
> greater than
< = less than or equal
> = greater than or equal
= equal to
<> not equal

For example, the expression

IF X > = Y GOTO 1100

means that if the value of X is (either) greater than or equal to the value of Y, then control branches to statement 1100.

A variable name is the name of a specific location in which a value is stored. It is called a "variable" because the value that is stored may be changed (or varied) during execution of the program. There are very specific rules for the name of a variable, which can be defined as one of two types: numeric or alphameric.

Numeric Variables contain only values with numeric digits that can be used in arithmetic. Numeric variables are named with a single alphabetic character, which *may* be followed by a single numeric digit (e.g., A, B3, but not 3B or BB), or (LET A = 147.5).

Alphameric Variables contain strings of alpha and numeric characters that are for reference only, such as a name or address. All characters are acceptable. Alphanumeric variables are named with a single alphabetic character followed by a dollar sign (e.g., A$, X$, but not $A), or (LET A$ = '143 MAIN ST').

Both numeric and alphameric variables have two categories: simple and array.

Simple   Each variable contains only one value; e.g., (LET A = 100; LET B$ = 'CDC 7600').

Array   Groups of values are stored under one variable name. The easiest way to understand an array is to think of it as a table with rows and columns. If the table has only one column, it is called a "list" and only one dimension (number of rows) is stated: DIM T(15) means that T is a list of 15 values, and you may refer to the third value in the list as T(3) or T(R) when R is equal to 3.

A table with 15 rows and 6 columns has two dimensions. For example: DIM T(15,6). You may refer to the third value in the sixth column as T(3,6) or T(R,C) when R is equal to 3 and C is equal to 6.

The use of ARRAYS (tables) significantly reduces the number of program statements necessary to accomplish many data processing procedures.

Numeric arrays are defined by a DIM statement with a single alphabetic character as the name. For example: DIM T(15,6)

Alphanumeric arrays are allowed only one column (one dimension) and are named by a letter and $. For example: DIM T$(15).

The remaining chapters will illustrate the use of the BASIC programming language to adapt a number of accounting functions to the computer.

QUESTIONS

1. Are both INPUT and PRINT examples of output type statements?
2. How many different statements can assign a value to a variable?
3. If a table is sometimes called a "list," how many columns does it have?
4. A single dimension array can be called a list. True _____ False _____?
5. What does <> mean?
6. What value will print in the following program?

```
100 Let X = 5
110 Let Y = 7
120 Let Z = X + Y * 2
130 PRINT Z
140 END
```

7. How can you insert parentheses in line 120 to change the printed result to 24?

4

GENERAL LEDGER SYSTEMS

Basic Objective: To know the general steps in the design and programming of a General Ledger system.

Specific Learning Objectives

1. To know the fundamental steps in a computer General Ledger system.
2. To know the statements necessary in a detailed Trial Balance Report program.
3. To be able to enter transactions into a computerized General Ledger system.
4. To understand the necessity for editing transactions for accuracy.
5. To be able to post transactions to the General Ledger file.
6. To be able to prepare a detailed Trial Balance Report.

THE GENERAL LEDGER

The General Ledger is a record of the balances of each of the accounts of a business and of the transactions to the accounts. The "Chart of Accounts" is arranged to provide a means of classifying the transactions into meaningful categories for reporting and analysis.

In a manual system, each account may appear on separate pages of the ledger. Each page is separated into two parts. The left side is referred to as the *debit* side, where all debit transactions to the account are listed. The right side is the *credit* side, where credit transactions to the account are listed.

Transactions are usually posted to the General Ledger on a periodic basis. This may be daily for a business with a very large volume of transactions. For a less active business it may be monthly or quarterly. Whatever the posting period, a Trial Balance must be taken upon completion of the posting to assure that the General Ledger is "in balance."

It is a fundamental accounting principle that the General Ledger must always be in balance; that is, the total of all accounts with debit balances must equal the total of all accounts with credit balances. The General Ledger may be out of balance if errors were made during posting. Common posting errors include:

1. Failure to post all transactions.
2. Posting a debit transaction as a credit.
3. Posting a credit transaction as a debit.
4. Posting the wrong amount of the transaction.
5. Posting the transaction to the wrong account.

These errors must be located and corrected before reports prepared from the General Ledger can show the real financial position of the firm.

COMPUTERIZING THE GENERAL LEDGER

Computers are used widely for General Ledger accounting. They classify and record a large volume of transactions in a relatively short period of time and easily handle the repetitive nature of General Ledger processing.

The General Ledger records are stored as a data file, probably called the "General Ledger" (Master) file. Each record contains:

1. Account number.
2. Account name.
3. Current account balance.

Additional information may be stored for each account, depending upon the reporting needs of the business. Control records are often inserted into the General Ledger file after groups of accounts that may be used to distinguish report categories for the financial statements (e.g., ASSETS).

Account balances are still represented as debit or credit. A widely used method of representing a credit is to store the amount as a negative figure and to store a debit amount as a positive figure. The summation of the General Ledger account balances (the Trial Balance) should therefore be zero; that is, the positive debits offset the negative credits, resulting in the total of zero.

A computerized accounting system requires strict controls. The General Ledger is the financial history of a business and therefore it is necessary that it remain accurate. It must always balance. Each group of transactions posted to it also must balance.

Before transactions to the General Ledger are posted, they must be edited (checked) to assure that they are accurate. Editing should verify that (1) the transactions are in balance (i.e., the total debits plus the total credits equal zero), and (2) that valid account numbers have been entered.

Upon completion of the editing, the transactions may be posted to the General Ledger file, after which a detailed Trial Balance Report should be produced. This shows the beginning balance of each account, the transactions posted to it, and the resulting balance. The Trial Balance must be printed to prove that the General Ledger balances (or does not balance).

STUDY OF THE GENERAL LEDGER SYSTEM

Objective. The purpose of the case study is to enter transactions to the computer, edit the transactions, post them to the General Ledger file, and prepare a detailed Trial Balance Report.

Background. The W. S. Wilson Company advises business firms on the design and installation of computer systems. The company is owned and managed by Mr. W. S. Wilson. Its revenues are generated by fees charged for the services of Mr. Wilson and his two employees.

The company utilizes time-sharing systems when developing and testing applications for its customers. It owns the computer terminals through which it accesses the time-sharing systems.

A summary Trial Balance prepared for April 19__ shows the accounts used by the company and the account balances. The Trial Balance is shown on page 32. The transactions occurring during May are listed on page 33.

The transactions are to be posted to the accounts listed. In addition, a brief description and a reference to the date or number of the source document from which the transaction originated are listed. This information aids in subsequent audits or inquiries into the status of the General Ledger accounts.

Explanation of the General Ledger System

The General Ledger system used by W. S. Wilson Company is used as an example, beginning on page 34. The explanation of the system includes:

1. A flowchart and description of the system, providing an overview. The flowchart is shown in Fig. 4.1.
2. A detailed description of the TRIBAL program, including a list of variables used (Table 4.1), flowcharts, and program coding.
3. Instructions and illustrations for using the system follow the TRIBAL program case study.

M. S. WILSON COMPANY
TRIAL BALANCE
April 19___

Account Number	Account Name	Debit Balance, $	Credit Balance, $
100	Cash	7000.00	
120	Accts. Receivable	8000.00	
150	Computer Equip.	9000.00	
155	Depreciation		1000.00
170	Program Copyrights	15000.00	
200	Accts. Payable		4500.00
220	Notes Payable		12000.00
230	Taxes Payable		3000.00
300	Wilson, Capital		13200.00
400	Fees Earned		40000.00
500	Salaries	16000.00	
510	Bad Debt Exp.	200.00	
520	Computer Exp.	14000.00	
530	Depr. Exp.	0.00	
540	Office Supplies	2000.00	
550	Travel & Entertain.	2000.00	
560	Utilities	500.00	
	Total	73700.00	73700.00

W. S. WILSON COMPANY
TRANSACTIONS
May 19___

Debit Acct.	Credit Acct.	Description	Source Ref.	Amount, $
500	100	Payroll Exp.	Pay. Reg. 2	3500.00
120	400	Fees to ABC Elect. Co.	Inv. 1135	2600.00
120	400	Fees to Owens Oil	Inv. 1136	4600.00
560	100	Pay't., utilities bill	Check 925	75.00
550	100	Travel Exp., Wilson	Check 926	125.00
220	100	Pay't. on note	Check 927	300.00
100	120	Pay't. from Smith Mfg.	Inv. 1120	2000.00
120	400	Fees to Jones Co.	Inv. 1137	500.00
100	120	Pay't. from Brown Ind.	Inv. 1118	4000.00
540	100	Purchase, office supplies	Check 928	300.00
200	100	Pay't., time-sharing inv.	Check 929	4000.00
550	100	Travel Exp., Smith	Check 930	75.00
100	120	Payment from ABC Elect.	Inv. 1135	2600.00
520	200	Rec. time-sharing inv.	Inv. 9237	6125

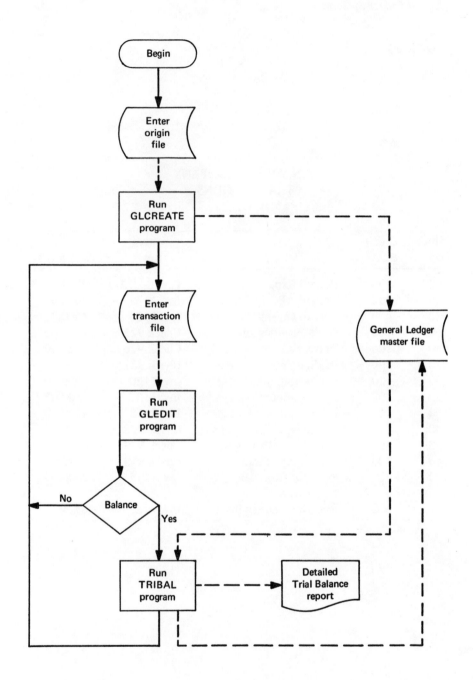

Fig. 4.1 Systems flowchart of a General Ledger accounting system.

34

THE COMPUTERIZED GENERAL LEDGER SYSTEM

The computerized General Ledger *system* includes three *programs*. Each program performs a specific function in the overall General Ledger system. They are defined as follows:

GLCREATE Program. This program creates the General Ledger (Master) file from an origin file of a company's accounts. The origin file BEGBAL already exists (see Appendix J) and contains the W. S. Wilson Co. account balances. Appendix K presents the GLCREATE Program.

GLEDIT Program. This program (Appendix L) edits each transaction record for a valid account number. It totals the transactions and prints the total after the last transaction has been edited. The total will be zero if the transactions are in balance.

TRIBAL Program. This program posts the transactions to the General Ledger file and prints the detailed Trial Balance. This program will be studied as an example of the programs comprising the system. The following examination of it shows the program design and coding necessary to post transactions to a General Ledger (Master) file and to print a detailed Trial Balance. Each procedure is described. The descriptions are illustrated by flowcharts and program coding.

THE TRIBAL PROGRAM CASE STUDY

Purpose. The TRIBAL program posts transactions to the General Ledger and prepares a detailed Trial Balance Report. The program flowchart is depicted in Fig. 4.2. Table 4.1 lists the variable names used in the program.

Note that the explanation of the program, which begins on page 38, is accompanied by the portion of the program flowchart that is applicable to the lines of the program shown on the facing page.

For example, the first column of the flowchart in Fig. 4.2 appears on page 38. That portion of the program produced from this section of the flowchart appears on the opposite page (page 39). This is followed by the second column of the flowchart, explanation of the lines, and the corresponding part of the program. Finally, the third column of the flowchart is shown and explained in the same manner. This third part of the program terminates the operations.

This method of presentation and explanation is generally adopted for other programs described in this and subsequent chapters.

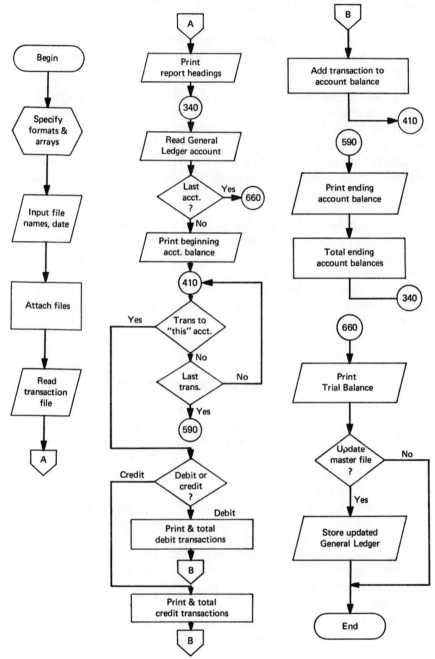

Fig. 4.2 TRIBAL program flowchart.

Table 4.1   Variable Names used in the TRIBAL Program

A(J)	General Ledger account number
N$(J)	General Ledger account name
B(J)	General Ledger account balance
E(I)	Transaction account number
D$(I)	Transaction description
R(I)	Transaction reference number
V(I)	Transaction amount
I	Count of number of transaction entries
J	Pointer to General Ledger account records
K	Pointer to transaction account records
T9	Trial Balance
T1	Total of debit transactions
T2	Total of credit transactions
G$	General Ledger file name
T$	Transaction file name
C$	Company name
Y$	Date of Trial Balance Report

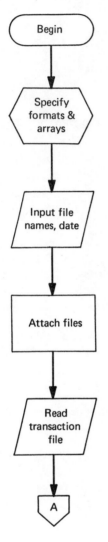

Lines 2–9 specify the print formats.
Line 20 specifies the size of arrays.

Lines 110–149 require the input of the General Ledger file name, the transaction file name, the company name, and the date of the report.

Lines 170–180 attach the General Ledger and transaction files to the program.

Lines 200–250 read the transactions from the transaction file. Each record contains the account number, a description, a reference to the source document, and the amount of the transaction. If the account number read in line 210 equals 999, the end of the file has been reached. Line 250 stores the count of the number of transactions entered.

```
1 REMARK: SPECIFY THE TRIAL BALANCE PRINT FORMATS
2:#################     GENERAL LEDGER TRIAL BALANCE     ################
3:ACCOUNT      ACCOUNT                                          ACCOUNT
4:NUMBER        NAME           REFERENCE     DEBIT     CREDIT    BALANCE
5: ###     #################      BEGINNING BALANCE            ######.##
6:         #################     #####     ######.##
7:         #################     #####               ######.##
8:                              ENDING BALANCE                 ######.##
9:         TRIAL BALANCE                 ######.## ######.##   ######.##
10   REMARK:  SPECIFY ARRAY SIZES
20        DIM A(50), N$(50), B(50), E(100), D$(100), R(100), V(100)
100 REMARK: INPUT FILE NAMES, COMPANY NAME, & DATE
110       PRINT 'ENTER GENERAL LEDGER MASTER & TRANSACTION FILE NAMES ';
120       INPUT G$,T$
130       PRINT 'ENTER COMPANY NAME ,   REPORT DATE ';
140       INPUT C$,Y$
160 REMARK: ATTACH FILES TO THE PROGRAM
170       OPEN 1, G$, INPUT
180       OPEN 2, T$, INPUT
190 REMARK: READ TRANSACTION FILE
200       LET I = I + 1
210       GET 2: E(I), D$(I), R(I), V(I)
220       IF E(I) = 999 GOTO 250
240       GOTO 200
250       LET I = I - 1
```

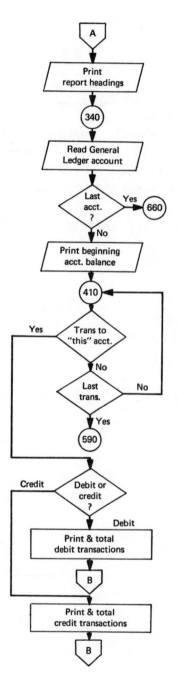

Lines 270–320 print the detailed Trial Balance Report headings.

Lines 340–370 read the accounts from the General Ledger file. A record with an account number of less than 100 signals the end of an account group (Assets, Liabilities, etc.) and is not printed. An account number of 999 signals that the end of the file has been reached.

Line 390 prints the beginning balance of the account.

Lines 410–450 check for transactions that apply to the General Ledger account currently being processed.

Line 470 determines if the transaction is a debit or a credit.

Lines 490–510 print and total all debit transactions.

Lines 530–540 print and total all credit transactions.

```
260 REMARK: PRINT HEADINGS FOR GENERAL LEDGER TRIAL BALANCE REPORT
270      PRINT
280      PRINT USING 2, C$, Y$
290      PRINT
300      PRINT USING 3
310      PRINT USING 4
320      PRINT
330 REMARK: READ ACCOUNT BEGINNING BALANCE FROM GENERAL LEDGER FILE
340      LET J = J + 1
350      GET 1: A(J), N$(J), B(J)
360      IF A(J) < 100 GOTO 340
370      IF A(J) = 999 GOTO 650
380 REMARK: PRINT ACCOUNT BEGINNING BALANCE
390      PRINT USING 5, A(J), N$(J), B(J)
400 REMARK: CHECK FOR TRANSACTIONS THAT APPLY TO "THIS" GL ACCOUNT
410      LET K = K + 1
420      IF E(K) = A(J) GOTO 460
440      IF K <= I GOTO 410
450      GOTO 580
460 REMARK: IF TRANSACTION AMOUNT IS NEGATIVE, IT IS A CREDIT
470      IF V(K) < 0 GOTO 530
480 REMARK: PRINT AND TOTAL DEBIT TRANSACTIONS
490      PRINT USING 6, D$(K), R(K), V(K)
500      LET T1 = T1 + V(K)
510      GOTO 550
520 REMARK: PRINT AND TOTAL CREDIT TRANSACTIONS
530      PRINT USING 7, D$(K), R(K), V(K)
540      LET T2 = T2 + V(K)
```

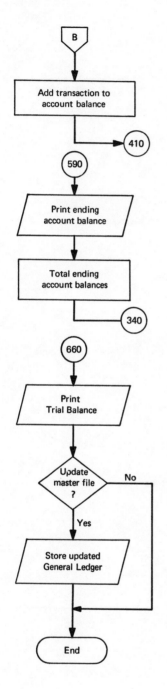

Line 560 adds the transaction amount to the account balance.

Lines 590–600 print the ending balance of the account.

Lines 620–640 add the ending account balances to the Trial Balance and return control to line 340.

Lines 660–690 print the total of the debit transactions, the total of the credit transactions, and the Trial Balance.

Lines 710–730 determine if the newly updated records are to be PUT in the General Ledger (Master) file, replacing the "previous" records.

Lines 750–800 will PUT the records in the master file.

Line 820 ends the program.

42

```
550 REMARK: POST TRANSACTION AMOUNT TO ACCOUNT BALANCE
560        LET B(J) = B(J) + V(K)
570        GOTO 410
580 REMARK: PRINT ENDING ACCOUNT BALANCE
590        PRINT USING 8, B(J)
600        PRINT
610 REMARK: TOTAL ENDING BALANCES OF ACCOUNTS (TRIAL BALANCE)
620        LET T9 = T9 + B(J)
630        LET K = 0
640        GOTO 340
650 REMARK: PRINT TRIAL BALANCE
660        PRINT
670        PRINT USING 9, T1, T2, T9
680        PRINT
690        PRINT
700 REMARK: DETERMINE IF MASTER FILE SHOULD BE UPDATED
710        PRINT 'DO YOU WISH TO UPDATE THE   GENERAL LEDGER FILE NOW ';
720        INPUT X$
730        IF X$ = 'NO' GOTO 820
735        IF X$ <> 'YES' GOTO 710
740 REMARK: STORE NEW GENERAL LEDGER RECORDS IN THE MASTER FILE
745        LET J = 0
750        OPEN 1, G$, OUTPUT
760        LET J = J + 1
770        PUT 1: A(J), N$(J), B(J)
780        IF A(J) = 999 GOTO 820
800        GOTO 760
820 END
```

INSTRUCTIONS FOR USING THE GENERAL LEDGER SYSTEM

Step 1. Sign onto the computer time-sharing system:

USER NUMBER, PASSWORD
▨▨▨▨▨▨▨▨▨▨▨▨▨▨▨▨▨▨▨▨▨▨▨▨▨▨▨▨▨ $\left(\begin{array}{l} \text{overprint retains} \\ \text{security} \end{array} \right)$

Step 2. Make an origin file including (1) line number, (2) account number, (3) account name, (4) beginning account balance. Be sure to use a unique name for the file. The origin data file for the W. S. Wilson Company has been prepared for you and is called BEGBAL. This file was entered as follows:

```
NAME BEGBAL
READY

100   100,    CASH                    ,      7000.00
110   120,    ACCTS.RECEIVABLE        ,      8000.00
120   150,    COMPUTER EQUIP.         ,      9000.00
130   155,       DEPRECIATION         ,     -1000.00
140   170,    PROGRAM COPYRIGHTS      ,     15000.00
150     1,    ASSETS                  ,         0.00
160   200,    ACCTS.PAYABLE           ,     -4500.00
170   220,    NOTES PAYABLE           ,    -12000.00
180   230,    TAXES PAYABLE           ,     -3000.00
190     2,    LIABILITIES             ,         0.00
200   300,    W.S.WILSON CAP.         ,    -13200.00
210     3,    CAPITAL                 ,         0.00
220   400,    FEES EARNED             ,    -40000.00
230     4,    INCOME                  ,         0.00
240   500,    SALARIES                ,     16000.00
250   510,    BAD DEBT EXPENSE        ,       200.00
260   520,    COMPUTER EXPENSE        ,     14000.00
270   530,    DEPR. EXPENSE           ,         0.00
280   540,    OFFICE SUPPLIES         ,      2000.00
290   550,    TRAVEL & ENTERTAIN      ,      2000.00
300   560,    UTILITIES               ,       500.00
310     5,    EXPENSE                 ,         0.00
999   999,    END                     ,         0.00

SAVE
READY
```

Notice that records have been inserted into the file after account groups, and that the value in the account number field corresponds to the first digit of the account numbers of the group. These records will be used in Chapter 5 to categorize the accounts for the financial statements.

Step 3. Run the GLCREATE program to create your General Ledger master file. Since you may be sharing the same user number with others doing these exercises, your data files must have unique names to be separate from the other users. An easy method is to incorporate your name into the names of your files. Your General Ledger file must be initialized before the program is RUN.

```
FILE GLWADE
READY

RUN GLCREATE

GLCREATE

ENTER NAME OF YOUR GENERAL LEDGER ORIGIN FILE   ? BEGBAL
ENTER NAME OF YOUR GENERAL LEDGER MASTER FILE   ? GLWADE

YOUR GENERAL LEDGER BEGINNING TRIAL BALANCE IS    0.00

PROCESSING    0 UNITS
```

Step 4. Enter the case study transactions into the computer. For each transaction, you must make two entries: one to the debit account and one to the credit account. Each entry consists of account number, description, reference number, and amount (the amount is negative for credit entries). Each transaction must also begin with a unique line number. Enter a record of

$$999\ 999\ ,0\ ,0\ ,0$$

after the last transaction.

```
NAME WADETRAN
READY

100  500,  PAYROLL                ,    2,   3500.00
110  100,  PAYROLL                ,    2,  -3500.00
120  120,  FEES-ABC ELECTRIC      , 1135,   2600.00
130  400,  FEES-ABC ELECTRIC      , 1135,  -2600.00

140  120,  FEES-OWENS OIL         , 1136,   4600.00
150  400,  FEES-OWENS OIL         , 1136,  -4600.00
160  560,  PYMT-UTILITIES         ,  925,     75.00
170  100,  PYMT-UTILITIES         ,  925,    -75.00
180  550,  TRAVEL-WILSON          ,  926,    125.00
190  100,  TRAVEL-WILSON          ,  926,   -125.00
200  220,  PAYMENT ON NOTE        ,  927,    300.00
210  100,  PAYMENT ON NOTE        ,  927,   -300.00
220  100,  REC-SMITH MFG.         , 1120,   2000.00
230  120,  REC-SMITH MFG.         , 1120,  -2000.00
240  120,  FEES-JONES COMPANY     , 1137,    500.00
250  400,  FEES-JONES COMPANY     , 1137,   -500.00
260  100,  REC-BROWN IND.         , 1118,   4000.00
270  120,  REC-BROWN IND.         , 1118,  -4000.00
280  540,  PUR.OFF.SUPPLIES       ,  928,    300.00
290  100,  PUR.OFF.SUPPLIES       ,  928,   -300.00
300  200,  PYMT-TIMESHARING       ,  929,   4000.00
310  100,  PYMT-TIMESHARING       ,  929,  -4000.00
320  550,  TRAVEL-SMITH           ,  930,     75.00
330  100,  TRAVEL-SMITH           ,  930,    -75.00
340  100,  REC-ABC ELECTRIC       , 1135,   2600.00
350  120,  REC-ABC ELECTRIC       , 1135,  -2600.00
360  520,  INV.-TIMESHARING       , 9237,   6125.00
370  200,  INV.-TIMESHARING       , 9237,  -6125.00
999  999,  0                      ,    0,      0.00

SAVE
READY
```

Step 5. Run the GLEDIT program to edit your transactions for valid account numbers and to check that they balance. If you have entered invalid account numbers or if the sum of your transactions does not equal zero, you must correct your transactions and run the GLEDIT program again.

```
RUN GLEDIT

GLEDIT

ENTER THE NAME OF YOUR GENERAL LEDGER FILE?  GLWADE
ENTER THE NAME OF YOUR TRANSACTION FILE    ?  WADETRAN

 28   TRANSACTIONS ACCEPTED
TOTAL OF ALL TRANSACTIONS ACCEPTED IS         0.00

   PROCESSING      1 UNITS
```

Step 6. Run the TRIBAL program to post the transactions to the General Ledger, print the detailed Trial Balance, and update the General Ledger master file.

```
RUN TRIBAL

TRIBAL

ENTER GENERAL LEDGER, TRANSACTION FILE NAMES?  GLWADE , WADETRAN
ENTER COMPANY NAME, REPORT DATE?  W.S.WILSON COMPANY , MAY 31  19
```

W.S.WILSON COMPANY	GENERAL LEDGER TRIAL BALANCE			MAY 31 19	
ACCOUNT NUMBER	ACCOUNT NAME	REFERENCE	DEBIT	CREDIT	ACCOUNT BALANCE
100	CASH	BEGINNING BALANCE			7000.00
	PAYROLL	2		-3500.00	
	PYMT-UTILITIES	925		-75.00	
	TRAVEL-WILSON	926		-125.00	
	PAYMENT ON NOTE	927		-300.00	
	REC-SMITH MFG.	1120	2000.00		
	REC-BROWN IND.	1118	4000.00		
	PUR.OFF.SUPPLIES	928		-300.00	
	PYMT-TIMESHARING	929		-4000.00	
	TRAVEL-SMITH	930		-75.00	
	REC-ABC ELECTRIC	1135	2600.00		
		ENDING BALANCE			7225.00
120	ACCTS.RECEIVABLE	BEGINNING BALANCE			8000.00
	FEES-ABC ELECTRIC	1135	2600.00		
	FEES-OWENS OIL	1136	4600.00		
	REC-SMITH MFG.	1120		-2000.00	
	FEES-JONES COMPANY	1137	500.00		
	REC-BROWN IND.	1118		-4000.00	
	REC-ABC ELECTRIC	1135		-2600.00	
		ENDING BALANCE			7100.00
150	COMPUTER EQUIP.	BEGINNING BALANCE			9000.00
		ENDING BALANCE			9000.00
155	DEPRECIATION	BEGINNING BALANCE			-1000.00
		ENDING BALANCE			-1000.00
170	PROGRAM COPYRIGHTS	BEGINNING BALANCE			15000.00
		ENDING BALANCE			15000.00

200	ACCTS.PAYABLE	BEGINNING BALANCE		-4500.00
	PYMT-TIMESHARING	929 4000.00		
	INV.-TIMESHARING	9237	-6125.00	
		ENDING BALANCE		-6625.00
220	NOTES PAYABLE	BEGINNING BALANCE		-12000.00
	PAYMENT ON NOTE	927 300.00		
		ENDING BALANCE		-11700.00
230	TAXES PAYABLE	BEGINNING BALANCE		-3000.00
		ENDING BALANCE		-3000.00
300	W.S.WILSON,CAP.	BEGINNING BALANCE		-13200.00
		ENDING BALANCE		-13200.00
400	FEES EARNED	BEGINNING BALANCE		-40000.00
	FEES-ABC ELECTRIC	1135	-2600.00	
	FEES-OWENS OIL	1136	-4600.00	
	FEES-JONES COMPANY	1137	-500.00	
		ENDING BALANCE		-47700.00
500	SALARIES	BEGINNING BALANCE		16000.00
	PAYROLL	2 3500.00		
		ENDING BALANCE		19500.00
510	BAD DEBT EXPENSE	BEGINNING BALANCE		200.00
		ENDING BALANCE		200.00
520	COMPUTER EXPENSE	BEGINNING BALANCE		14000.00
	INV.-TIMESHARING	9237 6125.00		
		ENDING BALANCE		20125.00
530	DEPR. EXPENSE	BEGINNING BALANCE		0.00
		ENDING BALANCE		0.00
540	OFFICE SUPPLIES	BEGINNING BALANCE		2000.00
	PUR.OFF.SUPPLIES	928 300.00		
		ENDING BALANCE		2300.00
550	TRAVEL & ENTERTAIN	BEGINNING BALANCE		2000.00
	TRAVEL-WILSON	926 125.00		
	TRAVEL-SMITH	930 75.00		
		ENDING BALANCE		2200.00
560	UTILITIES	BEGINNING BALANCE		500.00
	PYMT-UTILITIES	925 75.00		
		ENDING BALANCE		575.00
	TRIAL BALANCE		30800.00 -30800.00	0.00

DO YOU WISH TO UPDATE THE GENERAL LEDGER MASTER FILE NOW ? YES

PROCESSING   2 UNITS

QUESTIONS

1. What is the General Ledger?
2. What is the purpose of the General Ledger Trial Balance?
3. Why must a General Ledger be "in balance"?
4. How are credits and debits represented in a computerized General Ledger?
5. List three common posting errors.

6. The General Ledger contains a minimum of three items for each account. What are these three items?
7. What are the two functions of the program GLEDIT?
8. What is the purpose of the program TRIBAL?
9. What is the function of line 470 of the program TRIBAL?
10. What is the function of line 560 of the program TRIBAL?

PROBLEMS

1. Following the instructions given, run the case study as follows:
   (a) Using the GLCREATE program, establish the W. S. Wilson Company General Ledger file on the computer.
   (b) Enter and store the May transactions on the computer.
   (c) Run the GLEDIT program to edit the transactions.
   (d) Run the TRIBAL program to post the transactions to your General Ledger file, print a detailed Trial Balance, and update your General Ledger file.

2. In June, one computer terminal was sold by the W. S. Wilson Company at its current value of $2,000. It was replaced by a larger and more powerful terminal. This terminal was purchased for $4,000. Mr. Wilson paid $500 in cash and financed the remaining on a long-term note. These and other transactions for June were recorded as follows:

Debit Account	Credit Account	Description	Source Ref.	Amount, $
100	150	Sale of Term.	Rec. 501	2000.00
150		Purchase of Term.	Inv. 11319	4000.00
	100	Down Payment on Term.	Check 931	500.00
	220	Note, Bal. of Term.	Inv. 11319	3500.00
500	100	Payroll Exp.	P/R Reg. 2	3450.00
550	100	Entertain., Wilson	Check 932	35.00
100	120	Payment from Owens Oil	Inv. 1136	4550.00
120	400	Fees to Electra Air Co.	Inv. 1138	3500.00
220	100	Payment on Note	Check 933	300.00
120	400	Fees to Carter Co.	Inv. 1139	1500.00
100	120	Payment from Allied Co.	Inv. 1125	1800.00
100	120	Payment from Jones Co.	Inv. 1137	500.00
560	100	Payment, Utilities Bill	Check 934	60.00
120	400	Fees to Jones Co.	Inv. 1140	1700.00
550	100	Travel, Dow	Check 935	50.00
200	100	Payment, Time-sharing Inv.	Check 936	6125.00
520	200	Rec. Inv. for Time-sharing	Inv. 9557	4050.00

   (a) Enter and store the June transactions on the computer.
   (b) Run the GLEDIT program to edit the transactions.

(c) Run the TRIBAL program to post the transactions to the General Ledger, to print the detailed Trial Balance, and to update your General Ledger file.

3. Depreciation of computer terminals at the W. S. Wilson Company is posted semiannually, in June and December. The depreciation amount for January through June is $150. *Required:*

(a) Prepare the necessary transaction entries in the General Ledger to reflect the depreciation of the terminals.

(b) Enter and store the depreciation transactions on the computer.

(c) Run the GLEDIT program to edit these transactions.

(d) Run the TRIBAL program to post the depreciation to the General Ledger, to print a revised Trial Balance, and to update your General Ledger file.

4. In *Introduction to Accounting* by Emerson O. Henke, the following information for the month of January is given for the Zee Company:

Jan. 31	Charles Zee invested $30,000 cash in a small coin-operated washateria.
Jan. 5	Equipment costing $20,800 was purchased for cash.
Jan. 6	Additional equipment costing $15,000 was purchased by signing a 6% mortgage note secured by all equipment owned.
Jan. 8	Coin collection boxes were emptied. Mr. Zee deposited the receipts amounting to $75 in the bank.
Jan. 10	Rent in the amount of $200 was paid covering the month of January.
Jan. 12	A bill was received for machine installation costs in the amount of $1,200. This amount should be added to the cost of equipment.
Jan. 15	Coin collection boxes were emptied. Mr. Zee deposited the receipts amounting to $300 in the bank.
Jan. 22	Coin collection boxes were emptied. Mr. Zee deposited the receipts amounting to $450 in the bank.
Jan. 31	Coin collection boxes were emptied. Receipts amounting to $700 were deposited in the bank.
Jan. 31	Utility bills amounting to $250 were paid.
Jan. 31	A bill in the amount of $100 covering advertising for the month of January was received.

Required:

(a) Construct a beginning General Ledger for the Zee Company: (1) Develop an account number and name for each account needed. (2) Enter the accounts and their initial balances onto the computer time-sharing system. You may wish to list the BEGBAL file as an illustration of the entry of the W. S. Wilson Company's initial General Ledger balances. Note that after each account group (Assets, Liabilities, etc.) a record has been inserted to correspond to the first digit of the preceding account numbers. Also note that credit balances have been entered as negative figures. (3) Run the GLCREATE program to establish your General Ledger file for the Zee company.

(b) Enter the above transactions onto the computer time-sharing system. Use the transaction date as the reference number.

(c) Run the GLEDIT program to edit the transactions.

(d) Run the TRIBAL program to post the transactions to the General Ledger, print a detailed Trial Balance report, and update your General Ledger file for the Zee Company.

5. Given that the cash account for the Smith Company has been assigned the number 100, prepare a flowchart for a program that will report from the monthly transaction file all cash disbursements by the company.

5

FINANCIAL REPORTS

Basic Objective. To know the general steps in preparing a Balance Sheet and an Income Statement from a computerized General Ledger.

Specific Learning Objectives:
1. To know the basic structure of a Balance Sheet.
2. To know the basic structure of an Income Statement.
3. To know the statements necessary in an Income Statement program.
4. To know the statements necessary in a Balance Sheet program.
5. To be able to prepare an Income Statement from a computer General Ledger file.
6. To be able to prepare a Balance Sheet from a computer General Ledger file.

FINANCIAL STATEMENTS

At the end of an accounting period, statements are prepared to show the results of the business activities for that period. These are generally called financial statements and include:

1. A Balance Sheet.
2. An Income Statement.

The Balance Sheet

The Balance Sheet reflects the financial position of the business at the close of business on the last day of the accounting period. It summarizes all asset, liability, and capital accounts. Its name is derived from the fundamental accounting equation:

$$ASSETS = LIABILITIES + CAPITAL$$

That is, total assets equal, or balance to, total liabilities plus total capital.

Assets are those items owned by the firm. Cash in the bank, accounts receivable, equipment and furniture are all assets. Total assets increase when

51

additional equipment is purchased on credit; they decrease when payment on an account payable is made; or they remain constant when furniture is purchased with cash.

Assets come from resources contributed by two groups: the creditors and the owners. The creditors have supplied goods or services to the business and require payment in return. They have claim to the assets of the business for the amount owed to them. Their claims are termed "liabilities." Accounts payable, notes payable, and unearned income are liabilities. If equipment is bought on an installment plan, assets are increased by the value of the equipment, but so are accounts payable, a liability. The equipment is not completely owned by the business until the supplier has been fully paid.

The amount the owners invested in the business is called "capital." Capital is the margin of assets over liabilities and is sometimes called "owner's equity." Profits add to capital, whereas losses reduce it. The amount of capital should be a positive value; if not, the business is insolvent and likely to go into bankruptcy unless the owners invest more capital in the business.

The Income Statement

The Income Statement reflects the operating results of a business over a period of time. It is composed of all income and all expense accounts.

The income comprises all sales revenues received by the business. Expenses include all costs incurred in generating sales and in operating the business. Salaries, advertising, rent, and utilities are all expenses generated by the business.

The final line of the Income Statement shows the remainder of income less expenses. If the business has had a favorable operating performance, the result is a profit (net income). However, if the expenses have been greater than the revenues, the result is a loss (net loss). The net income (or net loss) is entered into the capital section of the Balance Sheet to reflect the results of business operation for that period.

COMPUTERIZING FINANCIAL REPORTS

Computerized General Ledger systems do not stop with printing a detailed Trial Balance. Programs that print the Income Statement and the Balance Sheet are also written. These programs access the General Ledger (Master) file for the account information necessary for the respective reports.

Account numbers are assigned by the category in which the account will be grouped on the financial statements and also by the order in which the accounts are to appear on the statements. The programs that print the financial statements may, on this basis, easily select the accounts to be printed; by selecting them in the sequence in which they are stored on the General Ledger file, the programs print them in the correct order.

The program that prints the Balance Sheet must compute and report totals of the following account categories:

1. Assets.
2. Liabilities.
3. Capital.
4. Liabilities and Capital.

The program that prints the Income Statement must compute and report totals of income, expenses, and net income (total income less total expense).

As discussed in Chapter 4 on computerizing the General Ledger, credits may be represented as negative figures. It is a principle of accounting that liabilities, capital, and income normally have credit balances. Financial statements presented to the owners of the firm, other investors, and the general public must follow the formal traditions of financial reporting. People outside the computer center and the accounting department are not aware, and need not be aware, that the computer carries the credit balances as negative figures. Therefore, for reporting purposes, the account balances in liability, capital, and income accounts are multiplied by –1, which reverses the sign without changing the value. As a result of this –1 multiplication, these balances are printed on the reports as positive values.

STUDY OF THE FINANCIAL REPORTING SYSTEM

Objective. The purpose of this study is to prepare an Income Statement and a Balance Sheet from a computer General Ledger file.

Background. The W. S. Wilson Company prepares an Income Statement and a Balance Sheet at the end of each month's accounting period. The company's General Ledger is stored on the computer and financial reports are prepared from it.

In studying the company's "Chart of Accounts," discussed in Chapter 4, you found that the accounts were given numbers to correspond to the report categories. A range of account numbers was assigned to the groups (compare with the Wilson Trial Balance) as follows:

100	Assets
200	Liabilities
300	Capital
400	Income
500	Expenses

The General Ledger (Master) file contains a record after the last account of each group, which is used to signal to the report programs that the group total is to be printed. The account number field in this record contains the first digit of the account group (i.e., 1 after Assets and 2 after Liabilities).

Explanation of the Financial Reporting System

The following pages describe the Income Statement and the Balance Sheet reports used by the W. S. Wilson Company. The explanation of the system includes:

1. A flowchart (Fig. 5.1) and description of the company's financial reporting, providing an overview.
2. A detailed description of the Income Statement program (Fig. 5.2), INCSTMT, including a list of variables used (Table 5.1), flowcharts, and program coding.
3. A detailed description of the Balance Sheet program (Fig. 5.3), BALSHEET, including a list of variables used (Table 5.2), flowcharts, and program coding.
4. Instructions and illustrations for using the system.

The data used for the Income Statement and the Balance Sheet are those of the W. S. Wilson Company on which the TRIBAL program was based in Chapter 4. Starting with the Trial Balance of April 19__ and updating with the transactions for May 19__, the data used in the Income Statement and the Balance Sheet described in this chapter can be correlated if the reader wishes to do this as an exercise. Needless to say, all this information has been placed in computer storage.

In the later section on instructions for using the financial reports system, the development of the originating data into the computerized Income Statement and Balance Sheet provides the thread of continuity among all programs that produce the various reports required by a well-organized business operation. For convenience in tracing these data to the reports discussed in this chapter, the beginning accounts and transactions are repeated on page 55.

W. S. WILSON COMPANY

TRIAL BALANCE APRIL 19___

Account Number	Account Name	Debit Balance, $	Credit Balance, $
100	Cash	7000.00	
120	Acct. Receivable	8000.00	
150	Computer Equip.	9000.00	
155	Depreciation		1000.00
170	Program Copyrights	15000.00	
200	Acct. Payable		4500.00
220	Notes Payable		12000.00
230	Taxes Payable		3000.00
300	Wilson, Capital		13200.00
400	Fees Earned		40000.00
500	Salaries	16000.00	
510	Bad Debt Expenses	200.00	
520	Computer Expense	14000.00	
530	Depreciation Exp.	0.00	
540	Office Supplies	2000.00	
550	Travel & Entertain.	2000.00	
560	Utilities	500.00	
	Total	73700.00	73700.00

TRANSACTIONS MAY 19___

Debit Acct.	Credit Acct.	Description	Source Ref.	Amount, $
500	100	Payroll Exp.	Pay Reg. 2	3500.00
120	400	Fees to ABC Elec Co.	Inv. 1135	2600.00
120	400	Fees to Owens Oil Co.	Inv. 1136	4600.00
560	100	Pay't. utilities bill	Check 925	75.00
550	100	Travel Exp., Wilson	Check 926	125.00
220	100	Pay't. on note	Check 927	300.00
100	120	Pay't. from Smith Mfg.	Inv. 1120	2000.00
120	400	Fees to Jones Co.	Inv. 1137	500.00
100	120	Pay't. from Brown Ind.	Inv. 1118	4000.00
540	100	Purchase, office suppl.	Check 928	300.00
200	100	Pay't. time-sharing inv.	Check 929	4000.00
550	100	Travel Exp., Smith	Check 930	75.00
100	120	Pay't. from ABC Elec. Co.	Inv. 1135	2600.00
520	200	Rec. time-sharing inv.	Inv. 9237	6125.00

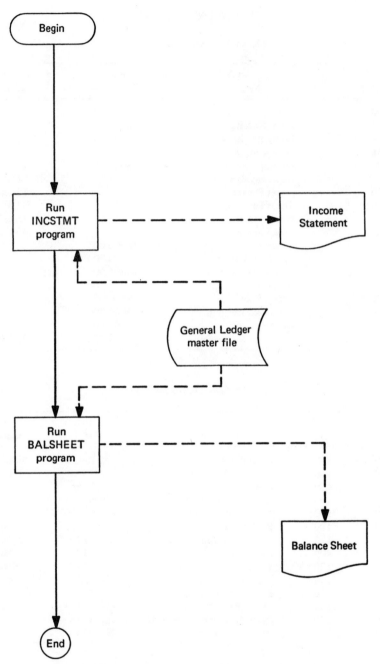

Fig. 5.1 Flowchart of a financial reporting system.

THE COMPUTERIZED FINANCIAL REPORTS

Two programs illustrate the computerized financial reports. Each program has been designed to print a specific report. The programs are defined as follows:

The INCSTMT Program

This program prepares an Income Statement. It calculates and prints total income, total expenses, and net income. Each procedure of the program is described. The descriptions are illustrated by flowcharts and program coding.

The BALSHEET Program

This program prepares a Balance Sheet. It calculates and prints total assets, total liabilities, total capital, and total liabilities and capital. Each procedure of the program is described. The descriptions are illustrated by flowcharts and program coding.

THE INCSTMT PROGRAM CASE STUDY

Purpose: The INCSTMT program prepares an Income Statement and calculates the company's net income.

The INCSTMT program flowchart is shown in Fig. 5.2. Table 5.1 lists the variable names used in the program.

TABLE 5.1   VARIABLE NAMES USED IN THE INCSTMT PROGRAM

G$	General Ledger file name
C$	Company name
D$	Date of the Income Statement report
A	General Ledger account number
N$	General Ledger account name
B	General Ledger account balance
I1	Total income
E1	Total expense
N1	Net income

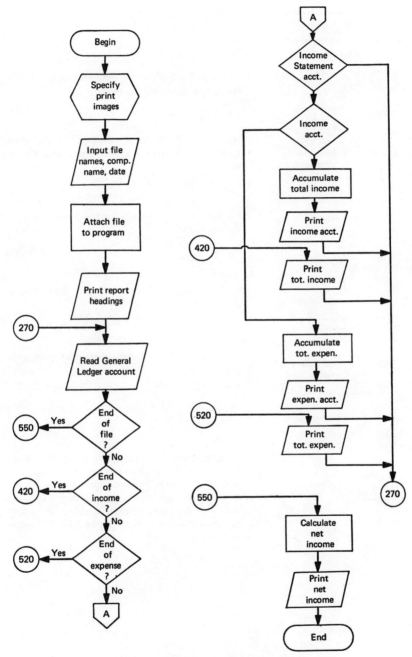

Fig. 5.2 INCSTMT program flowchart.

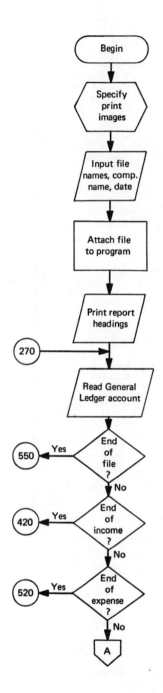

Lines 2–7 are the image statements that specify the print formats for the report.

Lines 110–140 require the input of the General Ledger file name, the company name, and the date of the report.

Line 160 attaches the General Ledger file to the program.

Lines 180–250 print the Income Statement report headings.

Lines 270–280 read the accounts from the General Ledger file. An account number of 999 signals that the end of the file has been reached.

Lines 300–310 determine if all the income accounts or all the expense accounts have been printed. If so, their respective total will be printed. A record with a 4 in the account number field follows the last income account; a record with a 5 in the account number field follows the last expense account.

```
1 REMARK: SPECIFY THE INCOME STATEMENT PRINT FORMATS
2:                        ##################
3:                        INCOME STATEMENT    ##################
4:  ACCOUNT NAME              ACCOUNT BALANCE
5:##################        ######.##
6:##################                           #######.##
7:                                             ==========
100 REMARK: INPUT FILE NAME, COMPANY NAME, REPORT DATE
110     PRINT 'ENTER YOUR GENERAL LEDGER FILE NAME';
120     INPUT G$
130     PRINT 'ENTER COMPANY NAME, REPORT DATE';
140     INPUT C$,D$
150 REMARK: ATTACH GENERAL LEDGER FILE TO THE PROGRAM
160     OPEN 1, G$, INPUT
170 REMARK: PRINT INCOME STATEMENT HEADINGS
180     PRINT
190     PRINT USING 2, C$
200     PRINT USING 3, D$
210     PRINT
220     PRINT USING 4
230     PRINT
240     PRINT 'INCOME'
250     PRINT
260 REMARK: READ ACCOUNT FROM GENERAL LEDGER FILE
270     GET 1: A, N$, B
280     IF A = 999 GOTO 540
290 REMARK: DETERMINE IF ALL INCOME OR EXPENSES HAVE PRINTED
300     IF A = 4 GOTO 410
310     IF A = 5 GOTO 510
```

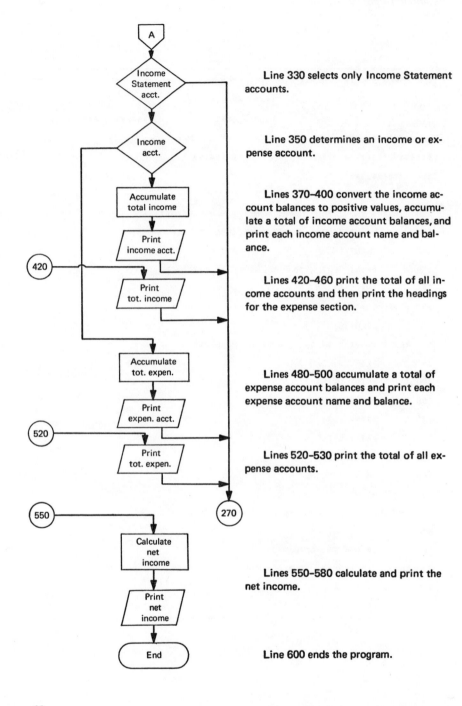

Line 330 selects only Income Statement accounts.

Line 350 determines an income or expense account.

Lines 370–400 convert the income account balances to positive values, accumulate a total of income account balances, and print each income account name and balance.

Lines 420–460 print the total of all income accounts and then print the headings for the expense section.

Lines 480–500 accumulate a total of expense account balances and print each expense account name and balance.

Lines 520–530 print the total of all expense accounts.

Lines 550–580 calculate and print the net income.

Line 600 ends the program.

```
320 REMARK: SELECT INCOME AND EXPENSE ACCOUNTS
330      IF A < 400 GOTO 270
340 REMARK: DETERMINE IF ACCOUNT IS AN EXPENSE
350      IF A >= 500 GOTO 470
360 REMARK: SET BALANCE TO POSITIVE, TOTAL AND PRINT INCOME ACCTS
370      LET B = B * (-1)
380      LET I1 = I1 + B
390      PRINT USING 5, N$, B
400      GOTO 270
410 REMARK: PRINT TOTAL INCOME
420      PRINT USING 6, 'TOTAL INCOME', I1
430      PRINT
440      PRINT 'EXPENSES'
450      PRINT
460      GOTO 270
470 REMARK: TOTAL AND PRINT EXPENSE ACCTS
480      LET E1 = E1 + B
490      PRINT USING 5, N$, B
500      GOTO 270
510 REMARK: PRINT TOTAL EXPENSES
520      PRINT USING 6, 'TOTAL EXPENSE', E1
530      GOTO 270
540 REMARK: CALCULATE AND PRINT NET INCOME
550      LET N1 = I1 - E1
560      PRINT
570      PRINT USING 6, 'NET INCOME', N1
580      PRINT USING 7
590 END
```

THE BALSHEET PROGRAM CASE STUDY

Purpose: The BALSHEET program prepares a company Balance Sheet. The BALSHEET program flowchart is shown in Fig. 5.3. Table 5.2 lists variable names used in the program.

TABLE 5.2   VARIABLE NAMES USED IN THE BALSHEET PROGRAM

G$	General Ledger file name
C$	Company name
D$	Date of the Balance Sheet report
A	General Ledger account number
N$	General Ledger account name
B	General Ledger account balance
N1	Net income from the Income Statement
A1	Total assets
L1	Total liabilities
C1	Total capital
T1	Total liabilities and capital

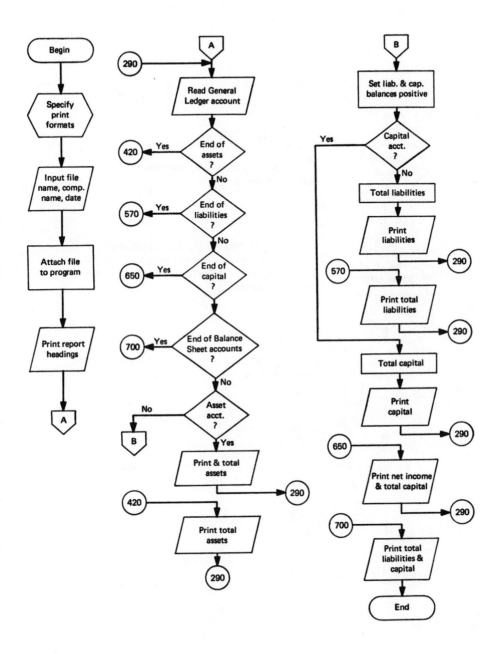

Fig. 5.3 BALSHEET program flowchart.

65

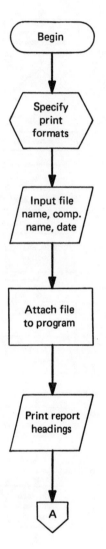

Lines 2–7 are the image statements that specify the print formats.

Lines 110–160 require the input of the General Ledger file name, the company name, the data of the report, and the net income printed on the income statement.

Line 180 attaches the General Ledger file name to the program.

Lines 200–270 print the Balance Sheet report headings.

```
1 REMARK: SPECIFY THE BALANCE SHEET PRINT FORMATS
2:                         ##################
3:                      BALANCE SHEET      ##################
4:  ACCOUNT NAME               ACCOUNT BALANCE
5:##################           ######.##
6:##################                           #######.##
7:                                             ==========
100 REMARK: INPUT FILE NAME, COMPANY NAME, REPORT DATE, NET INCOME
110       PRINT 'ENTER YOUR GENERAL LEDGER FILE NAME   ';
120       INPUT G$
130       PRINT 'ENTER COMPANY NAME, REPORT DATE';
140       INPUT C$,D$
150       PRINT 'ENTER NET INCOME FROM INCOME STATEMENT';
160       INPUT N1
170 REMARK: ATTACH GENERAL LEDGER FILE NAME TO PROGRAM
180       OPEN 1, G$, INPUT
190 REMARK: PRINT BALANCE SHEET HEADINGS
200       PRINT
210       PRINT USING 2,C$
220       PRINT USING 3,D$
230       PRINT
240       PRINT USING 4
250       PRINT
260       PRINT 'ASSETS'
270       PRINT
```

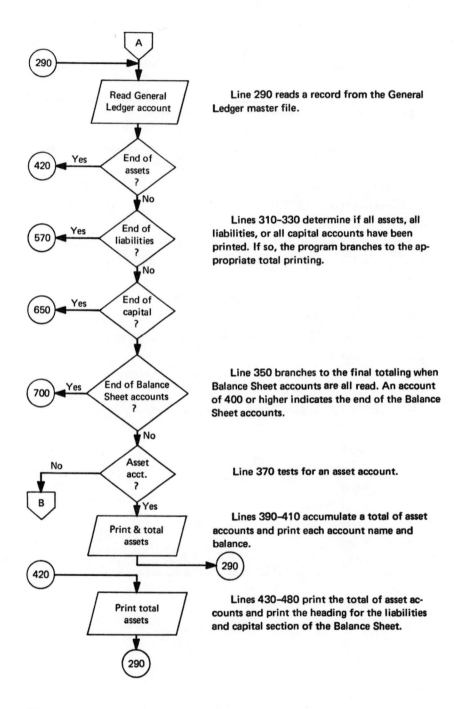

Line 290 reads a record from the General Ledger master file.

Lines 310–330 determine if all assets, all liabilities, or all capital accounts have been printed. If so, the program branches to the appropriate total printing.

Line 350 branches to the final totaling when Balance Sheet accounts are all read. An account of 400 or higher indicates the end of the Balance Sheet accounts.

Line 370 tests for an asset account.

Lines 390–410 accumulate a total of asset accounts and print each account name and balance.

Lines 430–480 print the total of asset accounts and print the heading for the liabilities and capital section of the Balance Sheet.

```
280 REMARK: READ ACCOUNT FROM GENERAL LEDGER FILE
290      GET 1: A, N$, B
300 REMARK: DETERMINE IF ALL ASSETS, LIAB OR CAPITAL HAVE PRINTED
310      IF A = 1 GOTO 420
320      IF A = 2 GOTO 570
330      IF A = 3 GOTO 650
340 REMARK: END OF BALANCE SHEET ACCOUNTS
350      IF A >= 400 GOTO 700
360 REMARK: DETERMINE IF ACCOUNT IS LIAB. OR CAPITAL
370      IF A >= 200 GOTO 490
380 REMARK: TOTAL AND PRINT ASSETS
390      LET A1 = A1 + B
400      PRINT USING 5, N$, B
410      GOTO 290
420 REMARK: PRINT TOTAL ASSETS
430      PRINT USING 6, 'TOTAL ASSETS', A1
440      PRINT USING 7
450      PRINT
460      PRINT 'LIABILITIES & CAPITAL'
470      PRINT
480      GOTO 290
```

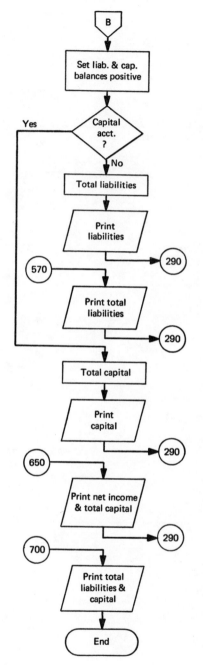

Line 500 converts the liability and capital account balances to positive values.

Line 520 determines if the account is a capital account.

Lines 540–560 accumulate a total of liability account balances and print each liability account name and balance.

Lines 580–600 print the total of all liability account balances.

Lines 620–640 accumulate a total of capital account balances and print each capital account name and balance.

Lines 660–690 print the net income from the Income Statement, add it to the total of capital, and print the total of capital plus net income.

Lines 710–760 add and print the total of liabilities and capital.

Line 770 ends the program.

```
490 REMARK: SET LIABILITIES & CAPITAL TO POSITIVE
500      LET B = B * (-1)
510 REMARK: DETERMINE IF ACCOUNT IS CAPITAL
520      IF A >= 300 GOTO 610
530 REMARK: TOTAL AND PRINT LIABILITIES
540      LET L1 = L1 + B
550      PRINT USING 5, N$, B
560      GOTO 290
570 REMARK: PRINT TOTAL LIABILITIES
580      PRINT USING 6, 'TOTAL LIABILITIES', L1
590      PRINT
600      GOTO 290
610 REMARK: TOTAL AND PRINT CAPITAL
620      LET C1 = C1 + B
630      PRINT USING 5, N$, B
640      GOTO  290
650 REMARK: PRINT NET INCOME, ADD TO CAPITAL AND PRINT TOTAL CAPITAL
660      PRINT USING 5, 'NET INCOME', N1
670      LET C1 = C1 + N1
680      PRINT USING 6, 'TOTAL CAPITAL', C1
690      GOTO 290
700 REMARK: CALCULATE AND PRINT TOTAL LIABILITIES AND CAPITAL
710      LET T1 = L1 + C1
720      PRINT
730      PRINT 'TOTAL LIABILITIES'
740      PRINT USING 6,' AND CAPITAL',T1
750      PRINT USING 7
770 END
```

INSTRUCTIONS FOR USING THE FINANCIAL SUPPORTS SYSTEM

Step 1. Sign onto the computer time-sharing system

USER NUMBER, PASSWORD
🅜🅜🅜🅜🅜🅜🅜🅜🅜🅜🅜🅜🅜🅜🅜🅜🅜🅜🅜🅜🅜🅜🅜🅜🅜🅜

Step 2. Run the INCSTMT program. You will be required to input your individual General Ledger file name, the name of the company, and report date for the Income Statement

```
RUN  INCSTMT

INCSTMT

ENTER YOUR GENERAL LEDGER FILE NAME?  GLWADE
ENTER COMPANY NAME, REPORT DATE?  W.S.WILSON COMPANY , MAY 31  19

                        W.S.WILSON COMPANY
                        INCOME STATEMENT       MAY 31  19

        ACCOUNT NAME              ACCOUNT BALANCE

   INCOME

   FEES EARNED                       47700.00
   TOTAL INCOME                                          47700.00

   EXPENSES

   SALARIES                          19500.00
   BAD DEBT EXPENSE                    200.00
   COMPUTER EXPENSE                  20125.00
   DEPR. EXPENSE                         0.00
   OFFICE SUPPLIES                    2300.00
   TRAVEL & ENTERTAIN                 2200.00
   UTILITIES                          575.00
   TOTAL EXPENSE                                         44900.00

   NET INCOME                                             2800.00
                                                        ==========


   PROCESSING       0 UNITS
```

Step 3. Run the BALSHEET program. You will be required to input your General Ledger file name, the name of the company, the date of the report, and the net income figure that was calculated and printed on the Income Statement.

```
RUN  BALSHEET

BALSHEET

ENTER YOUR GENERAL LEDGER FILE NAME   ?  GLWADE
ENTER COMPANY NAME, REPORT DATE?  W.S.WILSON COMPANY , MAY 31, 19
ENTER NET INCOME FROM INCOME STATEMENT? 2800.00
```

```
                        W.S.WILSON COMPANY
                        BALANCE SHEET           MAY 31  19

        ACCOUNT NAME            ACCOUNT BALANCE

        ASSETS

        CASH                      7225.00
        ACCTS.RECEIVABLE          7100.00
        COMPUTER EQUIP.           9000.00
          DEPRECIATION           -1000.00
        PROGRAM COPYRIGHTS       15000.00
        TOTAL ASSETS                              37325.00
                                                ==========

        LIABILITIES'& CAPITAL

        ACCTS.PAYABLE             6625.00
        NOTES PAYABLE            11700.00
        TAXES PAYABLE             3000.00
        TOTAL LIABLITIES                         21325.00

        W.S.WILSON CAP.          13200.00
        NET INCOME                2800.00
        TOTAL CAPITAL                            16000.00

        TOTAL LIABILITIES
          AND CAPITAL                            37325.00
                                                ==========

        PROCESSING      0 UNITS
```

QUESTIONS

1. What is a Balance Sheet?
2. What is an Income Statement?
3. What are the three major account groups on a Balance Sheet?
4. What are the two major sections of an Income Statement?
5. How is net income calculated?
6. What is the purpose of lines 300 and 310 of the INCSTMT program?
7. What is the purpose of line 370 of the INCSTMT program?
8. What is the purpose of line 350 of the BALSHEET program?
9. Which accounts conventionally have credit balances?

PROBLEMS

1. Following the instructions given in the case study and using the computer, prepare the following financial reports for the W. S. Wilson Company from the General Ledger file for May transactions, which was created in Chapter 4, Problem 1:
    (a) An Income Statement.
    (b) A Balance Sheet.
2. Prepare the financial reports for the W. S. Wilson Company from the

General Ledger file for June transactions, which was created in Chapter 4. These reports should reflect both the regular period entries that were posted to the file in Chapter 4, Problem 2, and the adjusting entries for depreciation that were posted to the file in Chapter 4, Problem 3. *Required:*

    (a) Prepare an Income Statement on the computer.

    (b) Prepare a Balance Sheet on the computer.

    3. Prepare the financial statements for the Zee Company from the General Ledger file for January transactions, which was prepared in Chapter 4, Problem 4. *Required:*

    (a) Run INCSTMT to prepare an Income Statement.

    (b) Run BALSHEET to prepare a Balance Sheet.

6

ACCOUNTS RECEIVABLE SYSTEMS

Basic Objective. To understand the general steps in the design and programming of an accounting system that is subsidiary to the General Ledger. Specifically, to understand how to design and program an Accounts Receivable system.

Specific Learning Objectives

1. To know the fundamental steps in a computer Accounts Receivable system.
2. To know the statements necessary in an Aged Accounts Receivable report.
3. To be able to enter transactions into a computerized Accounts Receivable system.
4. To be able to post the transactions to the Accounts Receivable file.
5. To be able to prepare an Aged Accounts Receivable report.
6. To know how to "write off" uncollectible invoices from the Accounts Receivable file.
7. To know how to add new customers to the Accounts Receivable file.
8. To know how to delete customers from the Accounts Receivable file.

SUBSIDIARY ACCOUNTING LEDGERS

The money owed to a business by its customers and the money owed by a business to its creditors must be accounted for in very accurate detail. Therefore, two subsidiary ledgers are generally maintained to itemize this information: the Accounts Receivable and Accounts Payable ledgers. Respectively, they account for the money owed to the firm and for the money that the firm owes to others.

The two ledgers are diametrical opposites. Both account for invoices by invoice number, date, and amount owed. The Accounts Receivable Ledger lists the customers of the business, and the Accounts Payable Ledger lists the vendors of goods and services to the business. To avoid repetition, only the

Accounts Receivable Ledger is discussed in this text. However, the principles applied to it also apply to a computerized Accounts Payable system.

The Accounts Receivable Ledger

The Accounts Receivable Ledger is subsidiary to the General Ledger. It lists each customer who owes money to the business and the amount he owes. The General Ledger maintains an Accounts Receivable account. However, this account reflects only the total of the Accounts Receivable Ledger. After posting all current activity to the Accounts Receivable Ledger, the total of the new invoices and the total of the payments collected are posted to the Accounts Receivable account in the General Ledger so that it remains balanced with the subsidiary ledger.

Advantages of detailing the customer information in a subsidiary ledger include (1) not overburdening the General Ledger with detail, and (2) maintaining greater control over the accounts receivable and their collection.

All purchases for which customers owe payment are listed in the Accounts Receivable Ledger. Generally each purchase is identified by:

1. Customer number.
2. Invoice number.
3. Invoice date
4. Amount of the invoice.

All invoices for a customer are grouped together. As payments are made, they are applied to the customer's outstanding invoices in one of two ways:

1. The amount paid is applied directly to the invoice for which the payment was made (open-item method).
2. The amount paid is applied to the oldest amounts due (balance-forward method).

A business selects the method most suited to its requirements. In both methods, the amounts due remain on the ledger until fully paid. We will use the open-item method in this chapter.

One of the primary purposes for maintaining an Accounts Receivable Ledger is to maintain control over the credit a business extends to its customers. A periodic Aged Accounts Receivable report should be prepared from the ledger. This report lists the total amount of Accounts Receivable and the amount owed by each customer. In addition, it categorizes the invoices by the length of time they have been due. Categorizing by length of time due is known as "aging." The common aging categories are:

1–30 days
31–60 days
61–90 days
Over 90 days

The Aged Accounts Receivable report helps the business to identify the payment habits of its customers. Based on information in the report, management decides to whom to extend credit or, if necessary, develops new policies to encourage faster payments by its customers.

The longer an invoice remains unpaid, the less probable that it will ever be paid. At some point, management must determine that the amount of the invoice is uncollectible and that it should be "written off," that is, credited in Accounts Receivable as a bad debt expense of the business. One method that may be used to record the bad debt write-off is to (1) delete the invoices from the Accounts Receivable Ledger; (2) credit the General Ledger Accounts Receivable account by the amount of the write-off, thus decreasing the balance of the account; and (3) debit the General Ledger Bad Debt Expense account by the amount of the write-off.

COMPUTERIZING THE ACCOUNTS RECEIVABLE LEDGER

The Accounts Receivable Ledger is maintained on the computer as a separate file from the General Ledger. After posting transactions to the Accounts Receivable file, summary totals of the transactions must also be posted to the General Ledger file.

Before an Accounts Receivable Ledger file is established on the computer, each customer is assigned a number by which the computer may reference them, allowing unpaid invoices to be stored on the computer and reported by customer number. The Accounts Receivable origin file is shown in Appendix M.

Transactions to the Accounts Receivable file will record either new sales invoices or payments received from customers. It is convenient to identify new invoices by entering the amount as a positive figure and to identify payments by entering the amount as a negative figure.

The Aged Accounts Receivable report categorizes the "ages" of the invoices on the master file by comparing their invoice dates to aging dates that the accountant supplies to the computer. These dates correspond to the age groups to be reported. For example, the invoices that appear in the 1–30 day category are dated during the current month; the invoices in the 31–60 day category are dated for the preceding month. If the report were to be prepared

at the end of August, all invoices with the month number 8 should appear in
the 1–30 day column, and the accountant would supply to the computer the
number 8 for use in determining which invoices were to be reported in this
column. He would also enter the month numbers for the other age categories.
The over-90 day column would include all invoices with month numbers prior
to those of the age categories supplied.

Many businesses label the first aging category (1–30 days) as "Current,"
since their credit terms allow 30 days after the invoice date for receipt of payment. In this case, they may label the second aging category as "1–30 days
overdue" and follow this concept with "31–60 days overdue" as the third
category. These different labels for the categories do *not* change the process
of aging the accounts receivable.

STUDY OF THE ACCOUNTS RECEIVABLE SYSTEM

Objective

The purpose of this case study is to enter transactions to the computer, post
the transactions to the Accounts Receivable file, prepare an Aged Accounts
Receivable report, write off uncollectible invoices from the Accounts Receivable file, and add or delete customers from the file.

Background

The Henry Flower Shop sells flowers to businesses and individuals. Many of
its customers make their purchases on credit. The shop maintains its Accounts
Receivable Ledger on the computer and receives a monthly Aged Accounts
Receivable report. The company's purpose in computerizing the Accounts
Receivable Ledger is to receive information that will enable it to control the
Accounts Receivable so that it will have a minimal number of accounts due
longer than 60 days. As payments are made on an account, the payment is
directly applied to the invoice specified. In the month of August, the follow-
ing transactions occurred to the Accounts Receivable Ledger.

Upon receipt of the Aged Accounts Receivable report, Mr. John Henry,
the owner of the shop, reviews all invoices over 90 days old. If an invoice is
determined to be uncollectible, it is deleted from Accounts Receivable and
expensed to Bad Debts. After receiving the August report, Mr. Henry determined that adjustments to the Accounts Receivable Ledger were necessary.

Date	Invoice	Customer Number	Customer Name	Charges	Payments
5/15	1065	100	Cafe Paris		75.75
8/2	1140	100	Cafe Paris	75.00	
8/2	1142	110	Drake Hotel	65.00	
8/5	1143	140	Kings Hotel	150.00	
6/10	1087	110	Drake Hotel		100.00
5/15	1071	170	Mrs. M. Peters		75.25
6/20	1102	170	Mrs. M. Peters		25.00
6/5	1082	170	Mrs. M. Peters		125.00
8/5	1144	140	Kings Hotel	250.00	
6/25	1105	190	Statewide Aero		100.00
8/10	1145	170	Mrs. M. Peters	125.00	
6/15	1100	220	Wilson Co.		60.60
8/15	1146	190	Statewide Aero	75.75	
8/15	1147	140	Kings Hotel	25.00	
7/15	1137	200	William Tucker		75.75
8/20	1148	150	Janice Long	25.00	
8/25	1149	120	State Bank	35.00	

These adjustments were made as follows:

1. The balance of the invoice to Mrs. M. Peters, dated April 15, is uncollectible.
2. The London Grill restaurant should be deleted from the ledger since it has selected another florist.
3. The Metropolitan Bank has signed a contract to receive its floral arrangements from the Henry Flower Shop. It has been assigned the customer number 230 and should be entered onto the master file.

Explanation of the Accounts Receivable System

The following pages describe the Accounts Receivable system used by the Henry Flower Shop. The explanation includes:

1. A flowchart (Fig. 6.1) and description, providing an overview.
2. A detailed description of the AGEREPT program, including a list of variables used (Table 6.1), flowcharts, and program coding.
3. Instructions and illustrations for using the system.

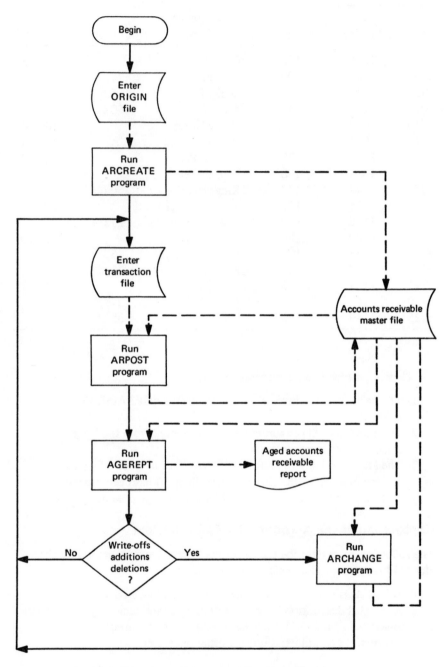

Fig. 6.1 Flowchart of the Accounts Receivable program.

THE COMPUTERIZED ACCOUNTS RECEIVABLE SYSTEM

The computerized Accounts Receivable system includes four programs. Each program performs a specific function in the overall system. They are defined as follows:

The ARCREATE Program

This program (Appendix N) creates an Accounts Receivable master file from an origin file. The origin file ARBEGIN already exists (Appendix M) and contains the required data for the Henry Flower Shop.

The ARPOST Program

This program (Appendix O) posts the Accounts Receivable transactions to the master file. Transactions may be rejected and not posted if (1) the customer is not in the master file; or (2) the invoice to which a payment is to be applied is not listed for the customer.

The AGEREPT Program

This program prints the Aged Accounts Receivable report. It requires entry of the month numbers that correspond to the age categories of the report. The program is described and is to be studied as an example of the programs comprising the system. The description is illustrated by flowcharts and program coding.

The ARCHANGE Program

This program (Appendix P) (1) deletes uncollectible invoices from the Accounts Receivable file, (2) adds new customers to the file, and (3) deletes customers from the file.

THE AGEREPT PROGRAM CASE STUDY

Purpose: The AGEREPT program prints the Aged Accounts Receivable report. The flowchart is shown in Fig. 6.2. Table 6.1 lists the variable names used in the program.

TABLE 6.1   VARIABLE NAMES USED IN THE AGEREPT PROGRAM

C	Customer number
N$	Customer name
X	Number of invoices on file for the customer
I	Invoice number
M	Invoice month number
D	Invoice day
A	Amount of the invoice
D1	1–30 day category month number
D2	31–60 day category month number
D3	61–90 day category month number
T	Total amount owed by a customer
T1	Total of the 1–30 day invoices of a customer
T2	Total of the 31–60 day invoices of a customer
T3	Total of the 61–90 day invoices of a customer
T4	Total of the over-90 day invoices of a customer
T5	Total of the Accounts Receivable file
T6	Total of all 1–30 day invoices
T7	Total of all 31–60 day invoices
T8	Total of all 61–90 day invoices
T9	Total of all over 90-day invoices
M$	Accounts Receivable Ledger file name
T$	Company name
Y$	Date of the Aged Accounts Receivable report

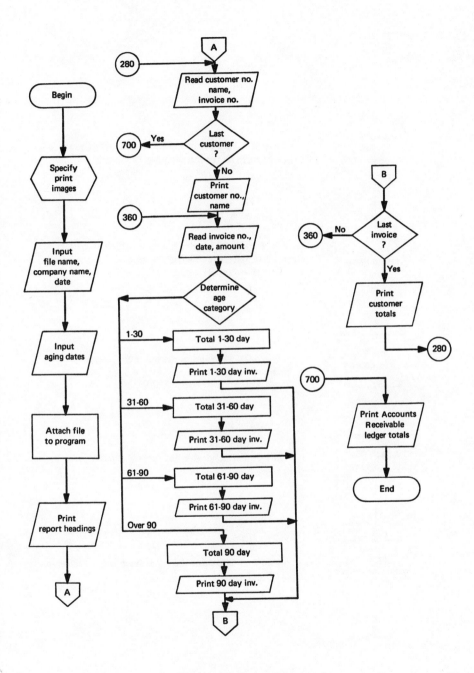

Fig. 6.2 AGEREPT flowchart.

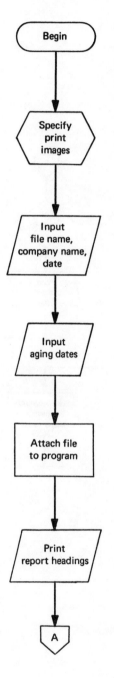

Lines 2–10 are the image statements that specify the print formats for the program.

Lines 100–140 require the input of the Accounts Receivable master file name, the company name, and the date of the report.

Lines 160–170 require the input of the month numbers to be used in determining the age categories.

Line 180 attaches the Accounts Receivable file to the program.

Lines 210–260 print the Aged Accounts Receivable report headings.

```
1 REMARK: PRINT IMAGES FOR AGED ACCT.REC. REPORT
2:################## AGED ACCOUNTS RECEIVABLE REPORT ##################
3 :CUSTOMER    INVOICE     1-30   31-60   61-90   OVER 90
4 :NO. NAME   NUMBER DATE  DAYS   DAYS    DAYS    DAYS    TOTAL
5 :### ###################
6 :          #### ##/## ####.##
7 :          #### ##/##         ####.##
8 :          #### ##/##                 ####.##
9 :          #### ##/##                         ####.##
10: TOTALS                ####.## ####.## ####.## ####.## ####.##
100 REMARK: INPUT ACCT.REC. MASTER FILE NAME, COMPANY NAME, DATE
110       PRINT 'ENTER ACCT.REC. MASTER FILE NAME';
120       INPUT M$
130       PRINT 'ENTER COMPANY NAME, REPORT DATE';
140       INPUT T$, Y$
150 REMARK: ENTER AGING DATES
160       PRINT 'ENTER MONTH NUMBERS FOR AGING';
170       INPUT D1, D2, D3
180 REMARK: ATTACH ACCT.REC. FILE TO PROGRAM
190       OPEN 1, M$, INPUT
200 REMARK: PRINT REPORT HEADINGS
210       PRINT
220       PRINT USING 2, T$, Y$
230       PRINT
240       PRINT USING 3
250       PRINT USING 4
260       PRINT
```

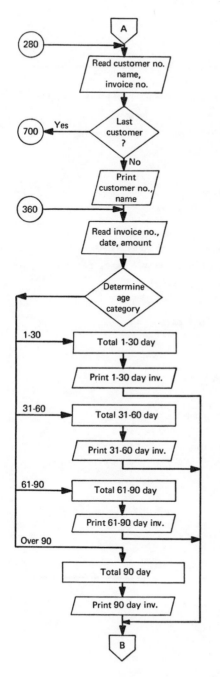

Line 280 reads a record from the Accounts Receivable master file, containing customer number, name, and number of invoices. A customer number of 999 will cause a branch to the final totaling statements.

Lines 310–320 print the customer number and name.

Lines 340–360 read the customer invoices from the file. If there are no invoices for a customer, the routine will be bypassed.

Lines 380–410 compare the invoice month to the aging months to determine the category under which the invoice should be printed.

Lines 430–450 print and total the 1–30 day invoices.

Lines 460–490 print and total the 31–60 day invoices.

Lines 500–530 print and total the 61–90 day invoices.

Lines 540–560 print and total the invoices over 90 days.

```
270 REMARK: GET CUSTOMER NUMBER, NAME, NUMBER OF INVOICES FROM FILE
280     GET 1: C, N$, X
290     IF C = 999 GOTO 690
300 REMARK: PRINT CUSTOMER NUMBER, NAME
310     PRINT
320     PRINT USING 5, C, N$
330 REMARK: READ INVOICES FOR CUSTOMER
340     IF X = 0 GOTO 600
350     LET L = 0
360     GET 1: I, M, D, A
370 REMARK: DETERMINE AGE CATEGORY TO PRINT INVOICE
380     IF M = D1 GOTO 420
390     IF M = D2 GOTO 460
400     IF M = D3 GOTO 500
410     GOTO 540
420 REMARK: PRINT AND TOTAL 1-30 DAY INVOICES
430     PRINT USING 6, I, M, D, A
440     LET T1 = T1 + A
450     GOTO 570
460 REMARK: PRINT AND TOTAL 31-60 DAY INVOICES
470     PRINT USING 7, I, M, D, A
480     LET T2 = T2 + A
490     GOTO 570
500 REMARK: PRINT AND TOTAL 61-90 DAY INVOICES
510     PRINT USING 8, I, M, D, A
520     LET T3 = T3 + A
530    *GOTO 570
540 REMARK: PRINT AND TOTAL ALL INVOICES OLDER THAN 90 DAYS
550     PRINT USING 9, I, M, D, A
560     LET T4 = T4 + A
```

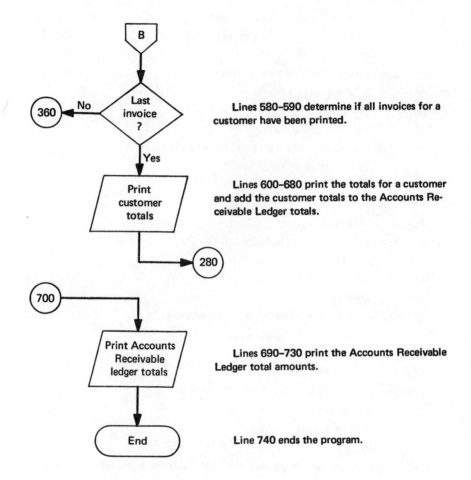

Lines 580–590 determine if all invoices for a customer have been printed.

Lines 600–680 print the totals for a customer and add the customer totals to the Accounts Receivable Ledger totals.

Lines 690–730 print the Accounts Receivable Ledger total amounts.

Line 740 ends the program.

```
570 REMARK: DETERMINE IF ALL INVOICES FOR CUSTOMER HAVE PRINTED
580      LET L = L + 1
590      IF L < X GOTO 360
600 REMARK: PRINT CUSTOMER TOTALS AND ADD TO ACCT.REC.LEDGER TOTALS
610      LET T = T1 + T2 + T3 + T4
620      PRINT USING 10, T1, T2, T3, T4, T
630      LET B1 = B1 + T1
640      LET B2 = B2 + T2
650      LET B3 = B3 + T3
660      LET B4 = B4 + T4
670      LET T1, T2, T3, T4, L = 0
680      GOTO 280
690 REMARK: PRINT ACCT.REC.LEDGER TOTALS
700      LET B = B1 + B2 + B3 + B4
710      PRINT
720      PRINT USING 10, B1, B2, B3, B4, B
740 END
```

INSTRUCTIONS FOR USING THE ACCOUNTS RECEIVABLE SYSTEM

Step 1. Sign onto the computer time-sharing system:

USER NUMBER, PASSWORD—

████████████████████████████████████

Step 2. Make an origin file, including a heading that describes each customer, and information on each of the invoices the customer has not paid. The heading includes (1) line number, (2) customer number, (3) customer name, (4) count of the number of invoices the customer has on file. The description of each invoice includes (1) line number, (2) invoice number, (3) invoice month, (4) invoice day, (5) amount of the invoice. Be sure to use a unique name for this file. The origin data file for the Henry Flower Shop has been prepared for you and is called ARBEGIN. The origin file was entered as follows:

```
NAME ARBEGIN
READY

100    100,     CAFE  PARIS              ,    3
110    1065,    5,    15,       75.75
120    1101,    6,    20,      100.05
130    1122,    7,     5,       75.95
140    110,     DRAKE  HOTEL             ,    3
150    1059,    4,    29,       50.00
160    1087,    6,    10,      100.00
170    1120,    7,     1,      150.50
180    120,     FIRST  STATE  BANK       ,    2
190    1107,    6,    25,       75.00
200    1133,    7,    15,       24.75
210    130,     HENRY  JONES             ,    2
220    1062,    5,    10,       75.25
230    1085,    6,     6,       50.00
240    140,     KINGS  HOTEL             ,    4
250    1066,    5,    15,      100.00
260    1080,    6,     5,       75.35
270    1112,    6,    25,      100.95
280    1130,    7,    15,      125.00
290    150,     JANICE  LONG             ,    1
300    1135,    7,    15,      150.00
310    160,     LONDON  GRILL            ,    0
320    170,     MRS.M.PETERSON           ,    6
330    1052,    4,    15,       55.00
340    1071,    5,    15,       75.25
350    1082,    6,     5,      125.00
360    1102,    6,    20,       35.00
370    1125,    7,    12,      125.35
380    1136,    7,    15,       90.00
390    180,     RUSTY  COMPANY           ,    3
400    1079,    5,    25,       25.35
410    1095,    6,    15,       75.00
420    1134,    7,    15,      100.00
430    190,     STATEWIDE  AIRLINES      ,    2
440    1105,    6,    25,      100.00
450    1131,    7,    15,      205.75
460    200,     WILLIAM  TUCKER          ,    1
470    1137,    7,    15,       75.75
480    210,     J.W.WASHINGTON           ,    1
490    1096,    6,    15,       25.00
```

```
500   220,   WILSON COMPANY     ,    3
510   1100,   6,   15,      60.60
520   1123,   7,    7,     120.00
530   1138,   7,   27,      70.25
999   999,   END               ,    0

SAVE
READY
```

Step 3. Run the ARCREATE program to create your Accounts Receivable master file. Your master file must be separate from that of anyone else who is doing these exercises. Incorporate your own last name in your master file name. The beginning balances of the case study are stored on the file ARBEGIN. Initialize your master file now!

```
FILE ARWADE
READY

RUN ARCREATE

ARCREATE

ENTER NAME OF YOUR ACCT.REC. ORIGIN FILE ? ARBEGIN
ENTER NAME OF YOUR ACCT.REC. MASTER FILE ? ARWADE

ACCOUNTS RECEIVABLE LEDGER TOTALS TO    2691.85
  13   CUSTOMERS ON ACCOUNTS RECEIVABLE FILE

PROCESSING      1 UNIT
```

Step 4. Enter the case study transactions into the computer. For each entry you must enter: customer number, invoice number, date (month, number, day), and the amount of the invoice. New invoices are entered with a positive amount figure; payments are entered with a negative amount figure. Each transaction must begin with a unique line number. Enter a record of

$$999\ 999,9,9,9,9$$

after the last transaction.

```
NAME WADEAR1
READY

100   100,   1065,   5,   15,    -75.75
110   100,   1140,   8,    2,     75.00
120   110,   1142,   8,    2,     65.00
130   140,   1143,   8,    5,    150.50
140   110,   1087,   6,   10,   -100.00
150   170,   1071,   5,   15,    -75.25
160   170,   1102,   6,   20,    -25.00
170   170,   1082,   6,    5,   -125.00
180   140,   1144,   8,    5,    250.00
190   190,   1105,   6,   25,   -100.00
200   170,   1145,   8,   10,    125.00
210   220,   1100,   6,   15,    -60.60
220   190,   1146,   8,   15,     75.75
230   140,   1147,   8,   15,     25.00
240   200,   1137,   7,   15,    -75.75
250   150,   1148,   8,   20,     25.00
260   120,   1149,   8,   25,     35.00
999   999,      9,   9,    9,      9.00

SAVE
READY
```

Step 5. Run the ARPOST program to post your transactions to the Accounts Receivable master file. Any transactions listed as rejected will not be posted. The totals for payments and for new invoices must later be posted to the Accounts Receivable account of the General Ledger file so that the balance of the account in the General Ledger equals the balance in the Accounts Receivable Ledger.

```
RUN ARPOST

ARPOST

ENTER ACCT.REC. MASTER FILE NAME, TRANSACTION FILE NAME? ARWADE, WADEAR1

TOTAL OF PAYMENTS POSTED               =   -637.35
TOTAL OF NEW INVOICES POSTED           =    826.25
TOTAL OF ACCOUNTS RECEIVABLE LEDGER FILE =  2880.75

DO YOU WISH TO UPDATE YOUR ACCT.REC. MASTER FILE NOW ? YES

PROCESSING      1 UNIT
```

Step 6. Run the AGEREPT program to print the Aged Accounts Receivable report. Enter the month numbers for August, July, and June as the dates for the aging categories.

```
RUN AGEREPT

AGEREPT

ENTER ACCT.REC. MASTER FILE NAME?  ARWADE
ENTER COMPANY NAME, REPORT DATE?  HENRY FLOWER SHOP , AUGUST 31  19
ENTER MONTH NUMBERS FOR AGING? 8, 7, 6

HENRY FLOWER SHOP  AGED ACCOUNTS RECEIVABLE REPORT AUGUST 31   19
```

CUSTOMER NO. NAME	INVOICE NUMBER	DATE	1-30 DAYS	31-60 DAYS	61-90 DAYS	OVER 90 DAYS	TOTAL
100 CAFE PARIS							
	1140	8/ 2	75.00				
	1101	6/20			100.05		
	1122	7/ 5		75.95			
TOTALS			75.00	75.95	100.05	0.00	251.00
110 DRAKE HOTEL							
	1059	4/29				50.00	
	1120	7/ 1		150.50			
	1142	8/ 2	65.00				
TOTALS			65.00	150.50	0.00	50.00	265.50
120 FIRST STATE BANK							
	1107	6/25			75.00		
	1133	7/15		24.75			
	1149	8/25	35.00				
TOTALS			35.00	24.75	75.00	0.00	134.75
130 HENRY JONES							
	1062	5/10			75.25		
	1085	6/ 6			50.00		
TOTALS			0.00	0.00	50.00	75.25	125.25

```
140 KINGS HOTEL
          1066   5/15                                    100.00
          1080   6/ 5                           75.35
          1112   6/25                          100.95
          1130   7/15                 125.00
          1143   8/ 5    150.50
          1144   8/ 5    250.00
          1147   8/15     25.00
     TOTALS             425.50       125.00    176.30    100.00    826.80
150 JANICE LONG
          1135   7/15                 150.00
          1148   8/20     25.00
     TOTALS              25.00        150.00      0.00      0.00    175.00
160 LONDON GRILL
     TOTALS               0.00          0.00      0.00      0.00      0.00
170 MRS.M.PETERSON
          1052   4/15                                     55.00
          1145   8/10    125.00
          1102   6/20                            10.00
          1125   7/12                 125.35
          1136   7/15                  90.00
     TOTALS             125.00        215.35     10.00     55.00    405.35
180 RUSTY COMPANY
          1079   5/25                                     25.35
          1095   6/15                            75.00
          1134   7/15                 100.00
     TOTALS               0.00        100.00     75.00     25.35    200.35
190 STATEWIDE AIRLINES
          1146   8/15     75.75
          1131   7/15                 205.75
     TOTALS              75.75        205.75      0.00      0.00    281.50
200 WILLIAM TUCKER
     TOTALS               0.00          0.00      0.00      0.00      0.00
210 J.W.WASHINGTON
          1096   6/15                            25.00
     TOTALS               0.00          0.00     25.00      0.00     25.00
220 WILSON COMPANY
          1123   7/ 7                 120.00
          1138   7/27                  70.25
     TOTALS               0.00        190.25      0.00      0.00    190.25
GRAND TOTAL             826.25       1237.55    511.35    305.60   2880.75

PROCESSING      1 UNIT
```

Step 7. Run the ARCHANGE program to delete invoice number 1052, the invoice that is uncollectible from Mrs. M. Peters. Also, delete London Grill from the file and add Metropolitan Bank as a new customer.

```
RUN ARCHANGE

ARCHANGE

ENTER ACCT.REC. MASTER FILE NAME?  ARWADE

ENTER CODE FOR TYPE OF CHANGE:
1=WRITE-OFFS; 2=NEW CUSTOMER; 3=DELETE CUSTOMER; 4=END
? 1
ENTER CUSTOMER, INVOICE FOR WRITE-OFF? 170,1052
```

```
ENTER CODE FOR TYPE OF CHANGE:
1=WRITE-OFFS; 2=NEW CUSTOMER; 3=DELETE CUSTOMER; 4=END
? 2
ENTER CUSTOMER NUMBER, CUSTOMER NAME? 230,'METROPOLITAN BANK'

ENTER CODE FOR TYPE OF CHANGE:
1=WRITE-OFFS; 2=NEW CUSTOMER; 3=DELETE CUSTOMER; 4=END
? 3
ENTER CUSTOMER NUMBER? 160

ENTER CODE FOR TYPE OF CHANGE:
1=WRITE-OFFS; 2=NEW CUSTOMER; 3=DELETE CUSTOMER; 4=END
? 4

TOTAL OF WRITE-OFF OF UNCOLLECTABEL INVOICES =     55.00
   1     NEW CUSTOMERS ADDED TO MASTER FILE
   1     CUSTOMERS DELETED FROM MASTER FILE

PROCESSING      1 UNIT
```

QUESTIONS

1. What is an Accounts Receivable Ledger?
2. What are two advantages of maintaining an Accounts Receivable Ledger apart from the General Ledger?
3. What four items entered onto the Accounts Receivable Ledger will describe a credit purchase made by a customer?
4. What is the purpose of an Aged Accounts Receivable report?
5. What are four common age categories on an Aged Accounts Receivable report?
6. What is the purpose of the program ARPOST ?
7. For what reasons might a transaction to the Accounts Receivable file be rejected?
8. What is the purpose of lines 380–410 of the program AGEREPT?
9. What steps are necessary to reflect the write-off of an uncollectible invoice in the Accounts Receivable Ledger and the General Ledger? (Describe each.)

PROBLEMS

1. Run the case study problem, following the instructions given:
   (a) Using the ARCREATE program, establish an Accounts Receivable file for the Henry Flower Shop.
   (b) Enter and store on the computer the Accounts Receivable transactions for August.
   (c) Run the ARPOST program to post the transactions to the Accounts Receivable file.

    (d) Run the AGEREPT program to prepare an Aged Accounts Receivable report.

    (e) Run the ARCHANGE program to make those changes in Accounts Receivable file that Mr. Henry has requested.

  2. In September, the following transactions were entered to the Henry Flower Shop Accounts Receivable Ledger:

Date	Invoice	Customer Number	Customer Name	Charges	Payments
9/5	1150	100	Cafe Paris	100.00	
7/7	1123	220	Wilson Co.		120.00
9/6	1151	140	Kings Hotel	55.00	
7/12	1125	170	Mrs. M. Peters		125.35
7/15	1136	170	Mrs. M. Peters		90.00
9/10	1152	170	Mrs. M. Peters	125.00	
5/25	1079	180	Rusty Co.		25.35
9/10	1153	200	William Tucker	85.75	
7/25	1135	150	Janice Long		150.00
9/15	1154	150	Janice Long	75.00	
6/25	1107	120	State Bank		75.00
9/15	1155	190	Statewide Aero	200.00	
5/10	1062	130	Henry Jones		75.25
9/20	1157	230	Metro Bank	250.00	
7/1	1120	110	Drake Hotel		150.50
9/25	1158	130	Henry Jones	65.00	
6/20	1101	100	Cafe Paris		100.05
5/15	1066	140	Kings Hotel		100.00
6/15	1095	180	Rusty Co.		75.00

Required:

    (a) Enter and store the September transactions on the computer.

    (b) Run the ARPOST program to post the transactions to the Accounts Receivable file.

    (c) Using the age categories of September, August, and July, run the AGEREPT program to prepare an Aged Accounts Receivable report.

  3. After reviewing the Aged Accounts Receivable report for September, Mr. Henry decided to write off invoice 1059 to the Drake Hotel, dated April 29, and the invoice 1096 to J. W. Washington, dated June 15. In addition, two new customers are added to the Accounts Receivable Ledger: the Republic Hotel (customer number 240) and the Smythe Company (customer number 250). *Required:* Run the ARCHANGE program to:

    (a) Delete the uncollectible invoices.

    (b) Add the two new customers.

  4. Develop a General Ledger file for the Henry Flower Shop and post the entries to it to reflect the Accounts Receivable transactions for September and the write-offs made in Problem 3. You must use the programs described in Chapter 4. *Required:*

    (a) First develop the General Ledger accounts necessary to record the company's Accounts Receivable activity; second, enter the accounts and their beginning balances onto the computer; and, third, run the GLCREATE program from Chapter 4 to create your General Ledger file.

    (b) Enter the transactions onto the computer.

    (c) Run the GLEDIT program to edit your transactions.

    (d) Run the TRIBAL program to post the transactions to the General Ledger and to print a detailed Trial Balance report.

7

PAYROLL ACCOUNTING SYSTEM

Basic Objective: To know the general steps in the design and programming of a business Payroll accounting system.

Specific Learning Objectives
1. To know the fundamental steps in a computer payroll system.
2. To know the statements needed in a weekly payroll program.
3. To be able to prepare a payroll register.
4. To be able to change an employee's payroll record.

STUDY OF THE PAYROLL ACCOUNTING SYSTEM

All businesses require some type of payroll accounting system. The employees expect to be paid on time and the U.S. Internal Revenue Service (IRS) requires that all employers maintain accurate records pertaining to employment taxes, including deductions of Federal income tax (FIT) and Social Security tax (FICA). The FIT and FICA deductions are withheld from the employees' earnings and are paid to the IRS. These and other applicable deductions constitute the difference between the gross pay earned and the net pay received. For accounting purposes, most businesses maintain payroll records on all employees. The records include (1) employee name, (2) employee identification number, (3) hours worked, (4) rate of pay, (5) gross pay, (6) taxes and other deductions, (7) year-to-date gross pay, taxes, and other deductions.

The computer time-sharing system provides the accuracy and control demanded by the time constraints of modern business and requires a minimum commitment of personnel and monetary resources. As illustrated in the following case study, the system is well suited to creating, maintaining, and executing a payroll accounting system for a small business as well as for a large one.

The payroll records may be called the Payroll Ledger, which is subsidiary to the General Ledger. The payroll totals such as gross pay, net pay, FIT withholding, and FICA withholding are included in the General Ledger and are posted for each pay period.

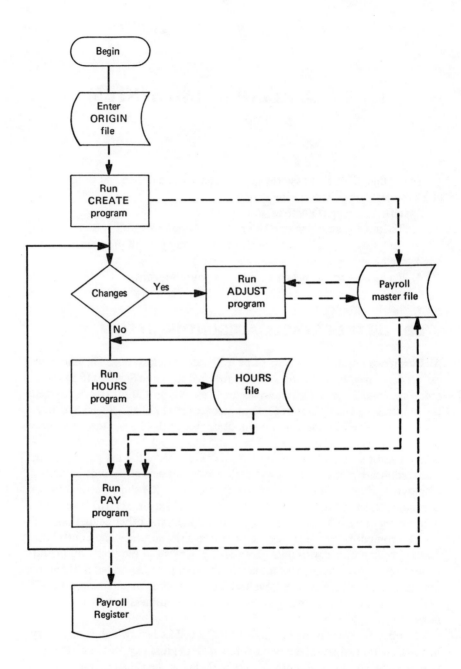

Fig. 7.1 System flowchart of computerized payroll system.

THE COMPUTERIZED PAYROLL SYSTEM

The computerized payroll system includes four programs. The system flow-chart is given in Fig. 7.1. Each program provides a specific function in the overall payroll system. They are defined as follows:

The CREATE Program

This program (Appendix Q) creates a payroll master file from an origin file (Appendix R).

The ADJUST Program

This program (Appendix S) makes adjustments and changes in a payroll master file. The primary uses of this program are to add new employees to the payroll and to make changes (e.g., number of tax deductions) in an employee record.

The HOURS Program

This program (Appendix T) creates a data file of the hours worked for each employee. It contains one record for each current employee, listing the employee number and number of hours worked. To insure accuracy and control, the program also checks for valid employee numbers and totals the hours entered.

The PAY Program

This program reads the payroll master file and the current week's hours file. It calculates current and year-to-date earnings and deductions of the employees. The program prints the Payroll Register and updates the payroll master file. The PAY program is to be studied as an example of the four programs comprising the system. The following examination of it shows the program design and coding required to produce a Payroll Register and to update the master file. A list of variables (Table 7.1) used in the program is provided for reference. Then each procedure is described and illustrated by a flowchart and by program coding.

THE PAY PROGRAM CASE STUDY

Purpose: The PAY program prepares a Payroll Register and an updated payroll master file.

Figure 7.2 depicts the PAY program flowchart. Table 7.1 lists the variable names used in the program.

TABLE 7.1   VARIABLE NAMES USED IN THE PAY PROGRAM

S(E)	Current week Social Security tax withheld.
C	Last employee number "found" in the master file.
Q2	Excess FICA earnings.
X(E)	Year-to-date net pay.
D$	Payroll closing date.
D(E)	Number of tax deductions.
F(E)	Current week Federal income tax withheld.
F$	Payroll master file name.
G(E)	Current week gross pay.
H(E)	Current week hours worked (becomes regular hours worked).
Y(E)	Year-to-date Federal income tax withheld.
M$(E)	Employee name.
L	Year-to-date gross pay through the prior week.
P(E)	Current week overtime hours.
R(E)	Regular pay rate.
V(E)	Year-to-date FICA withheld.
W(E)	Year-to-date gross pay.
N(E)	Current week net pay.
E	Employee number.
C1–C8	Payroll Register totals.

NOTE: An "E" within the parentheses following a variable name indicates the employee number during processing.

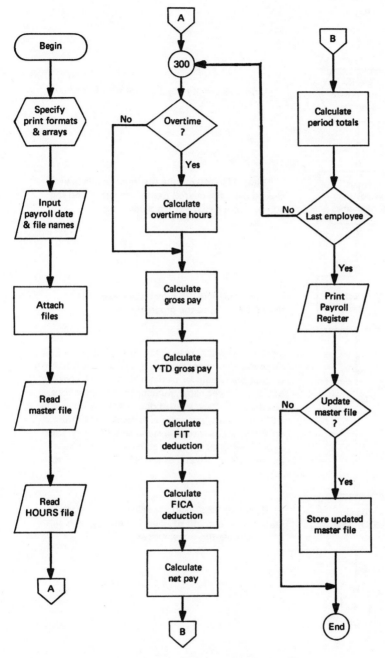

Fig. 7.2 PAY program flowchart.

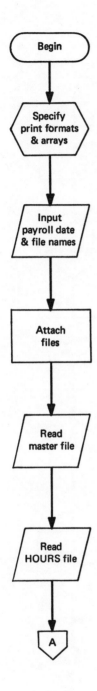

Lines 2–9 specify the print formats and arrays.

Lines 110–140 require the input of the payroll closing date, the payroll master file name, and the current week's HOURS file name.

Lines 160 and 170 attach the master file and the HOURS file to the program.

Lines 190–230 read in the master file. Line 190 reads the employee number. If it is not equal to zero, it reads the remainder of the record, which consists of the employee name, number of tax deductions, hourly rate of pay, year-to-date (ytd) gross pay, ytd FIT deductions, and ytd FICA deductions. If the employee number read in statement 190 *does* equal zero, it indicates that the end of the file has been reached. Then, reading of the HOURS file begins.

Lines 250–280 read the HOURS file, which contains the amount of hours worked by each employee during the current week.

```
1 REMARK:  SPECIFY THE PRINT FORMATS
2: ################## PAYROLL REGISTER   PERIOD ENDING ################
3: EMPLOYEE            WORK HOURS   GROSS        DEDUCTIONS        NET
4:NO.  NAME            REG  OVT     PAY        FIT     FICA        PAY
5:##  ################## ##.# ##.#  #####.##  #####.## #####.##  #####.##
6:     YTD TOTALS ->              #####.##  #####.## #####.## #####.##
7: WEEKLY TOTALS                  #####.##  #####.## #####.## #####.##
8         DIM M$(30), D(30), R(30), W(30), Y(30), V(30)
9         DIM  X(30), F(30), G(30), P(30), N(30), H(30), S(30)
100 REMARK:  FILE NAMES & PAYROLL DATE INPUT
105       PRINT 'ENTER COMPANY NAME ';
106       INPUT A$
110       PRINT 'ENTER THE PAYROLL CLOSING DATE ';
120       INPUT D$
130       PRINT 'ENTER PAYROLL MASTER FILE NAME AND HOURS FILE NAME';
140       INPUT F$,T$
150 REMARK:  THE FOLLOWING LINKS THE TWO FILES TO THE PROGRAM
160       OPEN 1, F$, INPUT
170       OPEN 3,T$,INPUT
180 REMARK:  MASTER FILE READ ROUTINE
190       GET 1: E
200       IF E = 0 GOTO 250
210       GET 1:  M$(E), D(E), R(E), W(E), Y(E), V(E)
220       LET C = E
230       IF C < 30 GOTO 190
240 REMARK:  CURRENT WEEK'S HOURS FILE READ ROUTINE
250       GET 3: E
260       IF E = 0 GOTO 290
270       GET 3:  H(E)
280       GOTO 250
285       REMARK:  E WILL BE 0 WHEN IT PASSES THIS POINT
```

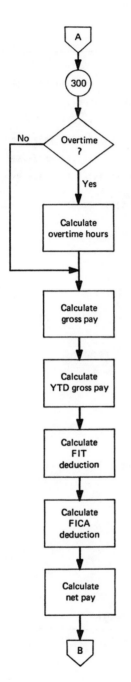

Lines 300–330 determine the amount of regular hours and overtime hours worked during the week. All time worked over 40 hours per week is considered overtime.

Line 350 calculates gross pay. Gross pay is the total of regular pay plus 1.5 times the pay rate for each hour of overtime.

Line 370 stores year-to-date gross pay prior to adding it to the current week's gross pay.

Lines 400–420 calculate FIT.

Lines 440–500 calculate FICA.

Lines 520 and 530 calculate the current week and year-to-date net pay by subtracting the deductions from the gross pay.

```
290 REMARK:    CALCULATION ROUTINE

295     REMARK: DETERMINE NO. OF REGULAR & OVERTIME HOURS

300       LET E = E + 1

310       IF H(E) <= 40 GOTO 340

320       LET P(E) = H(E) - 40

330       LET H(E) = 40

340     REMARK: GROSS PAY = ( REGULAR PAY )   + (   OVERTIME PAY   )

350           LET G(E) = ( H(E) * R(E) )   + ( P(E) * 1.5 * R(E) )

360     REMARK:  STORE YTD GROSS PAY FROM PREVIOUS PERIOD

370       LET L = W(E)

380       LET W(E) = W(E) + G(E)

390     REMARK:  CALCULATION OF FEDERAL INCOME TAX DEDUCTION

400       IF 13 * D(E) >= G(E) GOTO 430

410       LET F(E) = .18 * ( G(E)-.13 * D(E) )

420       LET Y(E) = Y(E) + F(E)

430     REMARK:  CALCULATE FICA (SOCIAL SECURITY DEDUCTION)

440       IF L >= 10800   GOTO 510

450       IF W(E) > 10800 GOTO 480

460       LET S(E) = 0.0585 * G(E)

470       GOTO 500

480       LET Q2 = W(E) - 10800

490       LET S(E) = 0.0585 * ( G(E) - Q2 )

500       LET V(E) = V(E) + S(E)

510     REMARK:  COMPUTE NET (TAKE HOME) PAY

520       LET N(E) = G(E) - ( F(E) + S(E) )

530       LET X(E) = W(E) - ( Y(E) + V(E) )
```

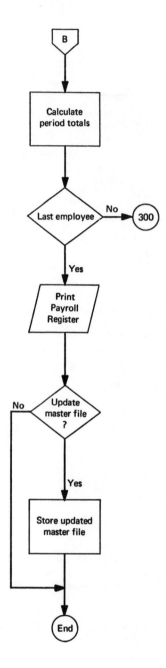

Lines 541–549 compute totals for the present period and year-to-date.

Line 550 determines if the current employee record is the last for the payroll calculations. If not, it returns control of the program to line 300 to calculate payroll information for the next employee.

Lines 560–690 print the Payroll Register headings and the payroll information for each employee. Line 650 prints the current week's data for each employee.

Line 660 prints the employee's year-to-date totals. Line 690 determines if the current employee record is the last to be printed on the Payroll Register. If not, it returns control of the program to line 640 to print the next employee record.

Lines 770–820 open the master file for output and write the new updated totals onto the file. Line 820 puts the zero end-of-file indicator into the file.

Line 830 ends the program.

```
541     REMARK:  SUM PAYROLL TOTALS
542       LET C1 = C1 + G(E)
543       LET C2 = C2 + F(E)
544       LET C3 = C3 + S(E)
545       LET C4 = C4 + N(E)
546       LET C5 = C5 + W(E)
547       LET C6 = C6 + Y(E)
548       LET C7 = C7 + V(E)
549       LET C8 = C8 + X(E)
550       IF E < C GOTO 300

555 REMARK: PRINTING OF RESULTS
560       REMARK:  SET  E=1  TO BEGIN ROUTINE WITH FIRST MAN
570       LET E = 1
580       PRINT
590       PRINT USING 2 , A$ , D$
600       PRINT
610       PRINT USING 3
620       PRINT USING 4
630       PRINT
640       IF G(E) = 0  GOTO 680
650       PRINT USING 5 , E, M$(E), H(E), P(E), G(E), F(E), S(E), N(E)
660       PRINT USING 6 ,                      W(E), Y(E), V(E), X(E)
670       PRINT
680       LET E = E + 1
690       IF E <= C  GOTO 640
695       PRINT USING 7 ,                      C1 ,  C2 ,  C3 ,  C4
697       PRINT USING 6 ,                      C5 ,  C6 ,  C7 ,  C8

700 REMARK: MASTER FILE UPDATE ROUTINE

710       LET E = 1

720       PRINT

730       PRINT'DO YOU WISH TO UPDATE YOUR MASTER FILE (' F$ ') NOW ';

740       INPUT A$

750       IF A$ = 'NO'  GOTO 830

760       IF A$ <>'YES'  GOTO 720

770       OPEN 2, F$,OUTPUT

780       PUT 2:  E, M$(E), D(E), R(E), W(E), Y(E), V(E)

790       LET E = E + 1

800       IF E <= C  GOTO 780

810       REMARK:  PUT 2: 0    IS THE END OF FILE INDICATOR

820       PUT 2: 0

830 END
```

INSTRUCTIONS FOR USING THE PAYROLL SYSTEM

Step 1. Sign onto the computer time-sharing system.

USER NUMBER, PASSWORD—
████████████████████████████████████

Step 2. Make an origin file of the employee's payroll data including (1) employee number, (2) name, (3) number of deductions, (4) hourly wage, (5) year-to-date gross pay, (6) year-to-date FIT, and (7) year-to-date FICA. The payroll origin file for the Rusty Manufacturing Company has been prepared for you and is called PAY1. It contains the following information:

```
100   1, HENRY WILLIAMS, 2,   3.75 ,  6125.00 , 1092.10 , 358.31
110   2, DONALD COOLEY , 1,   4.50 ,  8188.00 , 1468.64 , 479.00
120   3, RAYMOND HARRIS, 4,   3.25 ,  6080.00 , 1073.60 , 355.68
130   4, VINCENT HUMM  , 3,   3.50 ,  5250.00 ,  929.40 , 307.12
140   5, CARTER ZAPCO  , 2,   2.50 ,  4764.00 ,  847.12 , 278.69
150   6, FRANK KESTER  , 5,   5.25 , 10750.00 , 1909.00 , 628.87
160   7, PHYLLIS GISH  , 1,   3.10 ,  4920.00 ,  880.40 , 287.82
170   0
```

Step 3. Run the CREATE program to create your individual payroll master file. This program reads the origin data file and PUTs the required data into your payroll master file.

```
RUN CREATE

CREATE

ENTER THE NAME OF YOUR PAYROLL ORIGIN FILE ? PAY1
ENTER THE NAME OF YOUR PAYROLL MASTER FILE ? UPTON

7    PAYROLL MASTER RECORDS PUT IN FILE    : UPTON

PROCESSING      0 UNITS
```

Step 4. If any changes are to be made in the master file, the student runs the ADJUST program. The functions of this program are:

1. List the entire file.
2. Add a new employee record.
3. Delete an employee record from active pay status.
4. Make individual changes to a record.
5. Update the master file with the new changes.

```
RUN ADJUST

ADJUST

ENTER PAYROLL MASTER FILE NAME ? UPTON
USE FUNCTION CODE 88 FOR INSTRUCTIONS !

FUNCTION DESIRED ( 0 TO END )  ? 88

FUNCTIONS AVAILABLE ARE:
        1  LIST THE RECORDS IN THE FILE
        2  ADD A NEW EMPLOYEE RECORD
        3  DELETE AN EMPLOYEE RECORD
           FROM ACTIVE (PAY) STATUS.
        4  MAKE CHANGES TO A RECORD.
        5  UPDATE THE MASTER FILE (UPTON) WITH THE CHANGES

FUNCTION DESIRED ( 0 TO END )  ? 4

EMPLOYEE NO. ? 7

                                    < - - - YEAR TO DATE TOTALS - - - >
    EMPLOYEE            TAX  PAY    GROSS      DEDUCTIONS           NET
    NO.   NAME          DED  RATE    PAY      FIT      FICA         PAY
    (1)   (2)           (3)  (4)     (5)      (6)      (7)          (8)

     7  PHYLLIS GISH      1  3.10  4920.00  880.40  287.82  3751.78

IS THIS THE RIGHT EMPLOYEE ? YES

WHICH COLUMN (FIELD) TO BE CHANGED (2 THRU 7)
    ( 0 = NO MORE CHANGES )              ? 4

ENTER NEW PAY RATE ? 3.60

WHICH COLUMN (FIELD) TO BE CHANGED (2 THRU 7)
    ( 0 = NO MORE CHANGES )              ? 0

     7  PHYLLIS GISH      1  3.60  4920.00  880.40  287.82  3751.78

FUNCTION DESIRED ( 0 TO END )  ? 5
THE MASTER FILE (UPTON) IS UPDATED.

PROCESSING      1 UNITS
```

Step 5. Create the current week HOURS file by running the HOURS program. Enter a zero comma zero (0,0) after the last employee's hours have been entered.

```
RUN HOURS

HOURS

ENTER THE NAME OF YOUR PAYROLL MASTER FILE? UPTON
ENTER THE NAME OF YOUR HOURS FILE  ? CLARK

ENTER EMPLOYEE NUMBER, HOURS (0,0 TO END)
?  1,44
?  2,40
?  3,40
? 44,40
INVALID EMPLOYEE NUMBER. RE-ENTER
?  4,40
?  5,40
?  6,42
?  7,43
?  0,0

   7    EMPLOYEE HOURS ENTRIES PUT ON THE FILE  : CLARK
 289    TOTAL HOURS ENTERED.

PROCESSING      0 UNITS
```

Step 6. Now RUN the PAY program to calculate and print the Payroll Register and update the master file.

```
RUN PAY

PAY

ENTER COMPANY NAME ? RUSTY MFG CO.
ENTER THE PAYROLL CLOSING DATE ? 11/30/74
ENTER PAYROLL MASTER FILE NAME AND HOURS FILE NAME? UPTON,CLARK

   RUSTY MFG CO.        PAYROLL REGISTER    PERIOD ENDING 11/30/74

   EMPLOYEE            WORK HOURS     GROSS        DEDUCTIONS        NET
 NO.   NAME            REG   OVT       PAY        FIT      FICA       PAY

   1   HENRY WILLIAMS   40.0   4.0    172.50      31.00    10.09    131.41
         YTD TOTALS ->                6297.50   1123.10   368.40   4805.99

   2   DONALD COOLEY    40.0   0.0    180.00      32.38    10.53    137.09
         YTD TOTALS ->                8368.00   1501.02   489.53   6377.46

   3   RAYMOND HARRIS   40.0   0.0    130.00      23.31     7.60     99.09
         YTD TOTALS ->                6210.00   1096.91   363.28   4749.81

   4   VINCENT HUMM     40.0   0.0    140.00      25.13     8.19    106.68
         YTD TOTALS ->                5390.00    954.53   315.31   4120.16

   5   CARTER ZAPCO     40.0   0.0    100.00      17.95     5.85     76.20
         YTD TOTALS ->                4864.00    865.07   284.54   3714.38

   6   FRANK KESTER     40.0   2.0    225.75      40.52     2.92    182.31
         YTD TOTALS ->               10975.75   1949.52   631.80   8394.43

   7   PHYLLIS GISH     40.0   3.0    160.20      28.81     9.37    122.02
         YTD TOTALS ->                5080.20    909.21   297.19   3873.80

 WEEKLY TOTALS                       1108.45     199.10    54.56    854.79
       YTD TOTALS ->                47185.45    8399.36  2750.07  36036.03

DO YOU WISH TO UPDATE YOUR MASTER FILE (UPTON) NOW ? YES

PROCESSING      1 UNITS
```

QUESTIONS

1. The Rusty Manufacturing Corporation maintains a record of year-to-date earnings and deductions of all employees, even if the employee no longer works for the company. Why?
2. All business require some type of payroll accounting system. For accounting purposes, most businesses maintain payroll records on all employees. Generally, employee records are maintained in a Payroll Register. What five items are most often contained in a payroll register?
3. According to the payroll system flowchart, four programs are used in a payroll system. Name these four programs. Are all four programs run for each payroll period? Why?

4. What program would be used to change the hourly wage rate of an employee?
5. The PAY program creates a Payroll Register of the current and year-to-date earnings and deductions of the employees. What files are used as input to this program? Does this program modify any files? If so, which ones and how?
6. Referring to the PAY program flowchart:
   (a) What files are read into the PAY program?
   (b) Which file is read into the program first?
   (c) After the program calculates the employee net pay, what function is performed next?
7. Statement 210 in the PAY program reads an employee's record from the master file. Using the list of variable names used in the PAY program, identify the six variables read in from the master file.
8. Explain the purpose of lines 400–420 in the PAY program.
9. Referring to the flowchart in Fig. 7.1, answer these questions:
   (a) Does the HOURS program change the payroll master file?
   (b) What is the primary function of the HOURS program?

PROBLEMS

1. Create a payroll master file using the PAY1 origin file for the Rusty Manufacturing Company.

2. The hours worked for period 1 were as follows: employee 1, 40 hours; employee 2, 40 hours; employee 3, 42 hours; employee 4, 41 hours; employee 5, 40 hours; employee 6, 40 hours; employee 7, 43 hours. *Required:* Enter the hours listed, using the HOURS program, and produce a Payroll Register for period 1.

3. During pay period 2, Carter Zapro left the Rusty Manufacturing Company. Eldon Zick was hired to replace Mr. Zapro, and joined the company at an hourly rate of $2.75. Mr. Zapro left on a Monday morning and therefore did not earn any wages during that week's pay period. Mr. Zick and all other employees worked 40 hours during the week. *Required:* (a) Update your master file for period 2 to reflect the deleted and added employees using the ADJUST program. (b) Run the HOURS program to update the employees' HOURS file with the hours worked for the current pay period. (c) Run the PAY program to create a payroll register for the current pay period.

4. Donald Cooley worked 43 hours and Frank Kester worked 35 hours in pay period 3. All other employees worked a regular 40-hour week. *Required:* Update the weekly HOURS file and create a Payroll Register for pay period 3. What is the gross pay for Mr. Cooley and Mr. Kester for this period?

8

DEPRECIATION ACCOUNTING SYSTEMS

Basic Objectives. To be able to select the proper depreciation method and to be able to create a computerized depreciation schedule.

Specific Learning Objectives

1. To know the causes of depreciation.
2. To know the depreciation methods that are related to time.
3. To know the depreciation method that is related to an asset's use.
4. To know how to prorate partial-year depreciation.
5. To know how to calculate yearly accumulated depreciation.
6. To be able to prepare a sum-of-the year's digits depreciation schedule.
7. To be able to prepare a units-of-production depreciation schedule.
8. To be able to prepare a straight-line depreciation schedule.
9. To be able to prepare a declining-balance depreciation schedule.

STUDY OF THE DEPRECIATION ACCOUNTING SYSTEM

Assets having a productive or service life greater than a single accounting period and used in the production or sale of other assets or services are called "fixed assets." Since a fixed asset contributes to the production or sale of other assets for several periods, there needs to be a systematic procedure for amortizing the cost over its productive, or service, life. These procedures are defined as *depreciation methods*. This chapter discusses four depreciation methods.

1. Straight line.
2. Declining balance.
3. Sum of the digits (years).
4. Units of production.

Causes of Depreciation

Depreciation is the allocation of an asset's cost according to the revenues or benefits to be received from its use during each accounting period. When determining the proper depreciation method, it is important to consider the causes of depreciation. Causes of depreciation can be related to both use and the passage of time. Physical wear of an asset is a result of its use, and technological obsolescence due to newer inventions and technical improvements are related to the passage of time. Straight-line, declining-balance, and the sum-of-the digits depreciation methods are all related to the passage of time, and the units-of-production method is related to use. These methods are discussed in this chapter and a case study of each is presented.

Computing Depreciation

To compute a depreciation schedule, we must know (1) the cost of the asset, (2) its estimated useful life, and (3) its salvage value. The cost of a fixed asset includes the invoice price plus delivery charges and all costs incurred in preparing it for productive use, such as freight, trucking, power connections, and setup costs. The estimated useful life of an asset is the estimated period of time that the asset will be used in producing or selling other assets or services. The salvage value of an asset is the proportion of its cost estimated to be recoverable at the end of its useful life.

Partial-Year Depreciation. If an asset is acquired during the year, a partial first- and last-year depreciation charge may be computed, using the following formulas:

$$M = \text{number of months (first year) in use}$$
$$\text{First year depr} = M/12 \times \text{full first-year depreciation}$$
$$\text{Last year depr} = (12-M)/12 \times \text{full last-year depreciation}$$

These formulas allow us to prorate each full year's depreciation according to the number of months the asset is depreciated in the first and last years.

The following pages discuss the computerized depreciation accounting system. The flowchart illustrated (Fig. 8.1) includes four programs. Each program produces a specific type of depreciation schedule. The programs explained and described in this chapter are presented as case studies.

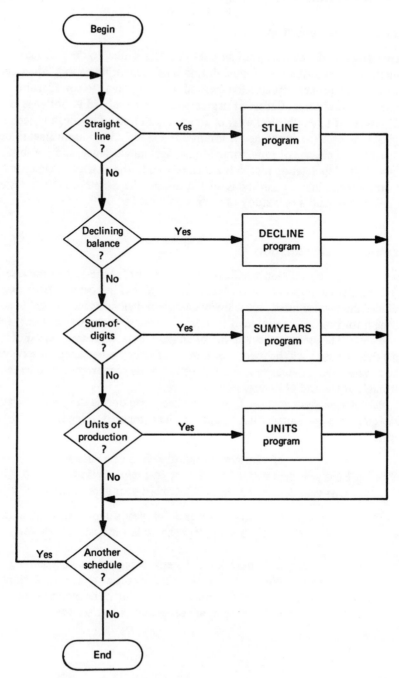

Fig. 8.1 System flowchart of the depreciation system.

THE COMPUTERIZED DEPRECIATION SYSTEM

The programs of the computerized depreciation system are defined as follows:

The STLINE Program

This program produces a yearly straight-line depreciation schedule.

The DECLINE Program

This program produces a yearly declining-balance depreciation schedule.

The SUMYEARS Program

This program produces a sum-of-the-digits (years) depreciation schedule.

The UNITS Program

This program produces a yearly units-of-production depreciation schedule.

All four programs use the same techniques to (1) input the cost, salvage value, and estimated life of an asset; (2) print the depreciation table heading; (3) calculate year-ending book value; (4) calculate year's accumulated depreciation; and (5) print the depreciation table values. The year-ending book value of an asset is calculated as the year's beginning book value minus the depreciation charge for that particular year. The year's accumulated depreciation is calculated as the accumulated depreciation for the preceding year (years) plus the current year's depreciation charge.

Each of the four depreciation methods and their corresponding descriptions, flowcharts, and programs are explained in subsequent sections. It should be noted that the flowcharts use some variable names and relate more closely to the program logic (see Table 8.2). These more technical flowcharts are presented as a contrast to those of previous chapters. Here, A:B means to compare the current value of these variables.

STRAIGHT-LINE DEPRECIATION METHOD

The straight-line depreciation method provides an equal depreciation charge per period. Because of its simplicity, the straight-line method is the most widely used depreciation procedure. The main disadvantages of using a straight-line procedure are that it does not account for changes in charges for repairs and maintenance, and that the operating efficiency of an asset decreases as it grows older. The straight-line depreciation method provides an equitable allocation of total depreciation charges if an asset is used about the same amount in each accounting period.

Calculating Straight-Line Depreciation

The straight-line depreciation procedure computes an equal depreciation charge per year by dividing the cost of an asset less its salvage value by the estimated number of years of its service life.

For example, using the straight-line method for determining a depreciation schedule on a machine costing $5,000, having an estimated salvage value of $2,600, and having an estimated life of three years, the yearly depreciation charge would be calculated as follows:

$$\frac{\text{Cost} - \text{salvage value}}{\text{Est. life in years}} = \frac{\$5,000 - 2,600}{3} = \$800$$

The yearly depreciation charge for the machine would be $800. The straight-line depreciation schedule that results is given in Table 8.1. The book value at the end of the third year is equal to the salvage value of the asset.

TABLE 8.1
THE STLINE DEPRECIATION SCHEDULE

Year	Book Value Beg. of Year, $	Annual Depreciation, $	Book Value End of Year, $
1	5,000	800	4,200
2	4,200	800	3,400
3	3,400	800	2,600

The STLINE Program

The STLINE program creates a straight-line depreciation schedule including:

1. Year number.
2. Book value of the asset at the beginning of the year.
3. Annual depreciation.
4. Accumulated depreciation.
5. Book value at the end of the current year.

The STLINE program also includes programming to calculate partial first- and last-year depreciation amortization. If an asset is acquired during the year, the program will prorate each full year's depreciation according to the number of months the asset is depreciated in the first and last year.

The following pages include a description, program flowchart, and illustration of the STLINE program. Table 8.2 lists the variable names used in this program. These names are also used in the three other programs. Cross reference to Table 8.2 is noted throughout.

TABLE 8.2
VARIABLE NAMES USED IN THE DEPRECIATION SYSTEM PROGRAMS

A	Cost of asset.
B	Beginning book value.
B1	Year-ending book value.
C	Counter for the number of years.
D	Yearly depreciation charge.
M	Number of months.
N$	Name of asset.
R	Yearly depreciation rate.
S	Salvage value of asset.
T	Yearly accumulated depreciation.
X	Sum of the digits (*only* in the SUMYEARS program).
Y	Number of years the asset is depreciated.
Y1	Counter for the number of years when the number of months in the first year is less than 12.
Z	Counter for the number of years in the depreciation schedule.

THE STRAIGHT-LINE PROGRAM CASE STUDY

Purpose: The STLINE program prepares a straight-line depreciation schedule. Figure 8.2 depicts the program flowchart. Refer to Table 8.2 for the variable names used in the program.

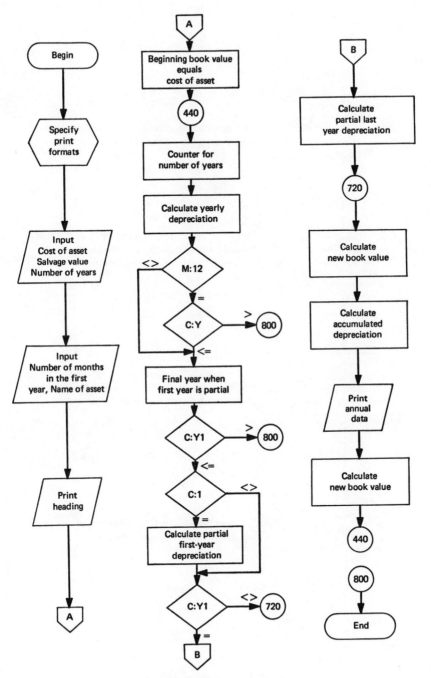

Fig. 8.2 STLINE program flowchart.

119

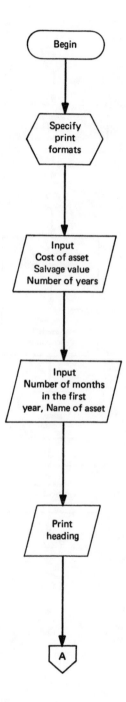

Lines 100–140 are the image statements that specify the print formats for the program.

Lines 150–240 require the input of the cost of the asset, the salvage value of the asset, and the number of years over which the asset will be depreciated.

Lines 250–310 require input of the number of months in the first year, over which the asset is to be depreciated, and the name of the asset.

Lines 320–400 print the heading of the straight-line depreciation schedule.

120

```
100 REMARK:  SPECIFY THE PRINT FORMATS
110:STRAIGHT LINE DEPRECIATION SCHEDULE FOR ###############
120:        BOOK VALUE      ANNUAL          ACCUMULATED    BOOK VALUE
130:YEAR    BEG. OF YR.     DEPRECIATION    DEPRECIATION   END OF YR.
140: ##     ########.##     #########.##    #########.##   #######.##
150 REMARK:  INPUT COST OF ASSET (A), SALVAGE VALUE (S),
160 REMARK:  AND NUMBER OF YEARS (Y)
170        PRINT 'STRAIGHT LINE DEPRECIATION METHOD'
180        PRINT
190        PRINT 'ENTER COST OF ASSET ';
200        INPUT A
210        PRINT 'ENTER SALVAGE VALUE ';
220        INPUT S
230        PRINT 'ENTER NO. OF YEARS  ';
240        INPUT Y
250 REMARK:  NO. OF MONTHS IN FIRST YEAR (M),
260 REMARK:  AND THE NAME OF THE ASSET (N$).
270        PRINT 'IN FIRST YEAR'
280        PRINT 'ENTER NO. OF MONTHS ';
290        INPUT M
300        PRINT 'ENTER NAME OF ASSET (LESS THAN 16 CHARACTERS) ';
310        INPUT N$
320 REMARK:  PRINTING OF HEADING
330        PRINT
340        PRINT
350        PRINT
360        PRINT USING 110, N$
370        PRINT
380        PRINT USING 120
390        PRINT USING 130
400        PRINT
```

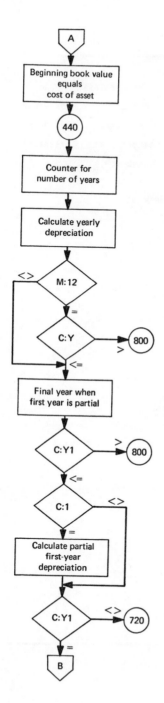

Lines 410–420 set the beginning book value of the asset equal to its cost.

Lines 430–440 cover the counter routine that determines the current year in the depreciation schedule.

Lines 450–460 calculate the straight-line depreciation; depreciation equals the cost of the asset less the salvage value divided by the total number of years over which the asset is to be depreciated.

Lines 470–490 test for a partial first year.

Lines 500–510 test to determine if the number of years completed in the depreciation schedule is less than, or equal to, the final year of the depreciation schedule. If it is, control is transferred to line 550.

Lines 520–530 transfer control to the end statement if the program is complete.

Lines 540–550 set the final year of the depreciation schedule equal to the estimated final year plus 1 only if the first year of the depreciation schedule is partial.

Lines 560–570 test to verify that the current year is less than, or equal to, the final year when the first year is partial. If so, control is transferred to line 610.

Lines 580–590 transfer control to line 800 if the schedule is complete and the first year is partial.

Lines 600–610 test to determine whether the counter is not equal to the first year. If it is not, control is transferred to line 660.

Lines 620–640 calculate first-year depreciation.

Lines 650–660 test to verify that the current year is not equal to the partial final year. If it is not, control is transferred to line 720.

```
410 REMARK:  SET BEGINNING BOOK VALUE EQUAL TO COST OF ASSET.
420       B = A
430 REMARK:  VARIABLE (C) IS USED AS A COUNTER FOR THE NUMBER OF YEARS
440       C = C + 1
450 REMARK:  (DEPRECIATION) = (COST OF ASSET - SALVAGE VALUE) / (YEARS)
460       LET    D        =     ( A      -      S )     /  ( Y )
470 REMARK:  TEST FOR PARTIAL FIRST YEAR
480 REMARK:  CONTROL TRANSFERRED TO 550 IF FIRST YR. IS PARTIAL.
490       IF M <> 12 THEN 550
500 REMARK:  CONTROL TRANSFERRED TO 550 IF NO. OF YRS. <= FINAL YR.
510       IF C <=  Y THEN 550
520 REMARK:  CONTROL TRANSFERRED TO END IF PROGRAM IS COMPLETE.
530       GO TO 800
540 REMARK:  (Y1) EQUALS THE FINAL YR. IF 1ST. YR. IS PARTIAL.
550       Y1 = Y + 1
560 REMARK:  IF SCHEDULE IS NOT FINISHED THEN CONTROL IS TRANS. TO 610.
570       IF C <= Y1 THEN 610
580 REMARK:  CONTROL IS TRANSFERRED TO END IF SCHEDULE IS COMPLETE.
590       GO TO 800
600 REMARK:  IF THE COUNTER <> 1ST. YR. THEN CONTROL IS TRANS. TO 660.
610       IF C <> 1 THEN 660
620 REMARK:  CALCULATION OF PARTIAL FIRST YEAR DEPRECIATION
630 REMARK:  ( 1 ST. YR. DEP. ) = ( NO. OF MTHS. / 12 ) * ( YRLY DEP. )
640       LET      D       = (     M     / 12.) * (       D     )
650 REMARK:  IF COUNTER <> FINAL YR. THEN CONTROL IS TRANS. TO 730.
660       IF C <> Y1 THEN 720
```

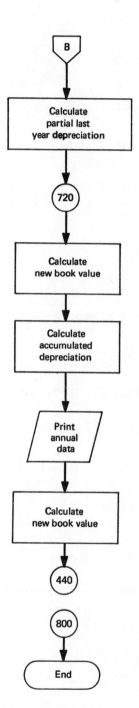

Lines 670–690 calculate the partial last-year depreciation: The partial last-year depreciation equals 1 minus the number of months in the first year, divided by 12, and multiplied by the yearly depreciation rate.

Lines 700–720 calculate the yearly ending book value of the asset: The ending book value equals the beginning book value of the current year minus the depreciation for the particular year.

Lines 730–740 calculate the accumulated depreciation: Accumulated depreciation equals the previously accumulated depreciation plus the current year's depreciation.

Lines 750–760 print the annual depreciation data, using the image statement in line 440.

Lines 770–780 set the beginning book value of the new year equal to the ending book value of the preceding year.

Line 790 returns control to line 440.

Line 800 ends the program.

```
670 REMARK:   CALCULATION OF PARTIAL LAST YR. DEPRECIATION
680 REMARK:   ( DEP. ) = ( 1 - ( MTHS. / 12. ) ) * ( YRLY DEP. )
690       LET    D    = ( 1 - ( M    / 12. ) ) * (    D    )
700 REMARK:   CALCULATION OF YRLY ENDING BOOK VALUE
710 REMARK:   ( END BOOK VAL ) = ( BEG BOOK VALUE ) - ( DEPRECIATION )
720       LET    B1     = (    B    ) - (    D    )
730 REMARK:   ( ACCUMULATED DEP. ) = ( OLD ACCUM. DEP. ) + ( DEP. )
740       LET    T     = (    T    ) + ( D  )
750 REMARK:   PRINTING OF ANNUAL DATA
760       PRINT USING 140, C, B, D, T, B1
770 REMARK:   END BOOK VAL OF PREVIOUS YR BECOMES BEG BOOK VAL OF NEW YR
780       B = B1
790       GO TO 440
800       END
```

Instructions for Using the STLINE Program

Step 1. Sign onto the computer time-sharing system:

USER NUMBER, PASSWORD—
█████████████████████████████

Step 2. Run the STLINE program to produce a straight-line depreciation schedule. Enter the (1) cost, (2) salvage value, (3) estimated life, and (4) name of the asset.

```
RUN STLINE

STLINE

STRAIGHT LINE DEPRECIATION METHOD

ENTER COST OF ASSET ? 140000
ENTER SALVAGE VALUE ?  20000
ENTER NO. OF YEARS  ?    10
IN FIRST YEAR
ENTER NO. OF MONTHS ?     5
ENTER NAME OF ASSET (LESS THAN 16 CHARACTERS) ? MACHINE#1205


STRAIGHT LINE DEPRECIATION SCHEDULE FOR MACHINE#1205
```

| | BOOK VALUE | ANNUAL | ACCUMULATED | BOOK VALUE |
YEAR	BEG. OF YR.	DEPRECIATION	DEPRECIATION	END OF YR.
1	140000.00	5000.00	5000.00	135000.00
2	135000.00	12000.00	17000.00	123000.00
3	123000.00	12000.00	29000.00	111000.00
4	111000.00	12000.00	41000.00	99000.00
5	99000.00	12000.00	53000.00	87000.00
6	87000.00	12000.00	65000.00	75000.00
7	75000.00	12000.00	77000.00	63000.00
8	63000.00	12000.00	89000.00	51000.00
9	51000.00	12000.00	101000.00	39000.00
10	39000.00	12000.00	113000.00	27000.00
11	27000.00	7000.00	120000.00	20000.00

```
PROCESSING    1 UNIT
```

SUM-OF-THE-DIGITS (YEARS) DEPRECIATION METHOD

This depreciation method provides a decreasing depreciation charge per period. It is generally applied to new assets that have fairly long lives. The advantage of the sum-of-the-year's digits depreciation method for long-lived fixed assets is that its application provides a more equitable "use" charge. Why? Because as an asset grows older, charges for repairs and maintenance increase and operating efficiency decreases. Therefore, a decreasing depreciation charge per period accompanied by increasing repair and maintenance charges provides a more equitable total expense charge to match against total revenues for each period.

Calculating Sum-of-the-Digits (Years) Depreciation

This depreciation procedure applies reducing rates to a constant base to obtain a decreasing charge per period.

The reducing rates are computed by adding together the years in the estimated service life of the asset and using this sum as the denominator in a series of fractions. The numerators of these fractions are the individual year numbers in asset life, but the year numbers are listed in reverse order.

For example, using the sum-of-the-digits method in determining depreciation on a machine costing $5,000, having an estimated salvage value of $1,500, and having an estimated life of four years, the denominator for the reducing rates is the sum of the digits, 1 through 4:

$$1 + 2 + 3 + 4 = 10$$

TABLE 8.3
CALCULATION OF SUMYEARS DEPRECIATION

Year	Book Value Beg. of Year, $	Base, $	Rate	Depreciation Charge, $	Book Value End of Yr., $
1	5000.00	3500.00	4/10	1400.00	3600.00
2	3600.00	3500.00	3/10	1050.00	2550.00
3	2550.00	3500.00	2/10	700.00	1850.00
4	1850.00	3500.00	1/10	350.00	1500.00

The numerators for the rates will be the year numbers in reverse order (4, 3, 2, 1), yielding the following fractions: 4/10, 3/10, 2/10, 1/10. Thus, using the depreciation base of $3,500 (cost less salvage value), annual depreciation charges can be calculated as shown in Table 8.3. Notice that the ending book value of the asset in the fourth year is equal to the salvage value of the asset.

The SUMYEARS Program

The SUMYEARS program creates a sum-of-the-digits depreciation schedule including:

1. Year number.
2. Book value at the beginning of the year.
3. Annual depreciation.
4. Accumulated depreciation.
5. Book value at the end of the current year.

This section includes a description, a program flowchart, and illustration of the SUMYEARS program.

THE SUMYEARS PROGRAM CASE STUDY

Purpose: The SUMYEARS program prepares a sum-of-the-years-digits depreciation schedule. Figure 8.3 depicts the program flowchart. The variable names listed in Table 8.2 also apply here.

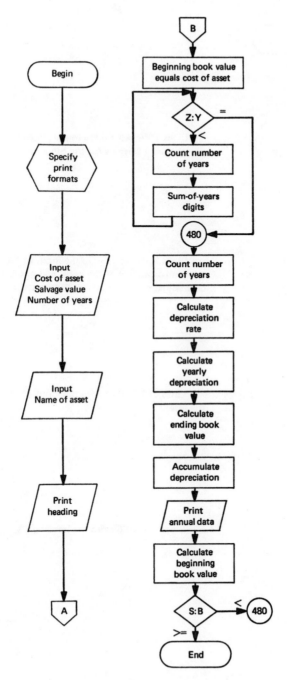

Fig. 8.3 SUMYEARS program flowchart.

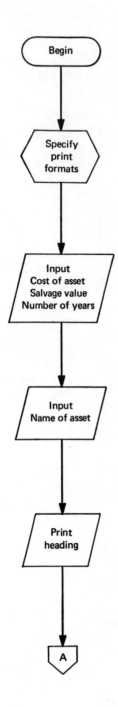

Lines 100–140 are the image statements that specify the print formats for the program.

Lines 150–240 require the input of the cost of the asset, salvage value of the asset, and number of years over which the asset is to be depreciated.

Lines 250–270 require the input of the name of the asset.

Lines 280–360 print the heading.

```
100 REMARK:  SPECIFY THE PRINT FORMATS
110:SUM OF THE YEARS DIGITS DEPRECIATION SCHEDULE FOR ###############
120:        BOOK VALUE      ANNUAL          ACCUMULATED    BOOK VALUE
130:YEAR    BEG. OF YR.     DEPRECIATION    DEPRECIATION   END OF YR.
140: ##     #########.##    #########.##    #########.##   #######.##
150 REMARK:  INPUT COST OF ASSET (A), SALVAGE VALUE (S),
160 REMARK:  AND NUMBER OF YEARS (Y)
170        PRINT 'SUM OF THE YEARS DIGITS DEPRECIATION METHOD'
180        PRINT
190        PRINT 'ENTER COST OF ASSET ';
200        INPUT A
210        PRINT 'ENTER SALVAGE VALUE ';
220        INPUT S
230        PRINT 'ENTER NO. OF YEARS  ';
240        INPUT Y
250 REMARK:  INPUT NAME OF THE ASSET
260        PRINT 'ENTER NAME OF ASSET (LESS THAN 16 CHARACTERS) ';
270        INPUT N$
280 REMARK:  PRINTING OF HEADING
290        PRINT
300        PRINT
310        PRINT
320        PRINT USING 110, N$
330        PRINT
340        PRINT USING 120
350        PRINT USING 130
360        PRINT
```

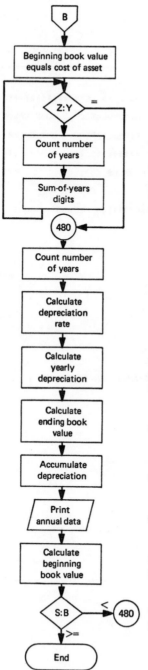

Lines 370–380 set the beginning book value of asset equal to the cost of the asset.

Lines 390–460 calculate the sum of the year's digits. Line 430 is a counter for the number of years used in the sum-of-the-year's digits calculation routine. Line 450 commands summation of the sum of year's digits in the calculation routine. Line 460 instructs the computer to return to line 390.

Lines 470–480 count the number of years in the depreciation schedule.

Lines 490–510 calculate the yearly depreciation rate.

Lines 520–540 calculate the amount of yearly depreciation: Depreciation equals rate calculated in line 570 times the value of the asset minus its salvage value.

Lines 550–570 calculate yearly ending book value.

Lines 580–600 calculate amount of yearly accumulated depreciation.

Lines 610–620 print the values in the depreciation table.

Lines 630–640 set the beginning book value of the new year equal to the book value of the previous year.

Line 660 tests to verify that the salvage value is less than the new book value. If so, the program branches to line 480.

Line 680 ends the program.

```
370 REMARK:   BEG BOOK VALUE = ( COST OF ASSET )
380       LET      B       = (      A      )
390 REMARK:   CALCULATION OF THE SUM OF THE YEARS DIGITS
400 REMARK:   IF Z = NUMBER OF YRS. THEN CONTROL IS TRANSFERRED TO 470
410       IF    Z =      Y          THEN       470
420 REMARK:   VARIABLE ( Z ) IS A COUNTER FOR THE YEARS
430      LET Z = Z + 1.
440 REMARK:   VARIABLE ( X ) IS A SUMMER FOR THE SUM OF THE YRS DIGITS
450      LET X = X + Z
460      GO TO 390
470 REMARK:   VARIABLE (C) IS USED AS A COUNTER FOR THE NUMBER OF YEARS
480      LET C = C + 1
490 REMARK:   CALCULATION OF THE YRLY DEPRECIATION RATE
500 REMARK:   RATE = ( YEARS - ( PRESENT YR - 1. ) ) / (SUM OF YRS)
510      LET  R = (    Y   - (     C     - 1. ) ) / (     X    )
520 REMARK:   CALCULATION OF THE YRLY DEPRECIATION
530 REMARK:   DEPRECIATION = (RATE) * (ASSET - SALVAGE VALUE)
540      LET      D      = ( R ) * ( A   -       S     )
550 REMARK:   CALCULATION OF YRLY ENDING BOOK VALUE
560 REMARK:   ( ENDING BOOK VAL ) = ( BEG BOOK VAL ) - ( DEPRECIATION )
570      LET       B1      = (      B      ) - (     D      )
580 REMARK:   CALCULATION OF YRLY ACCUMULATED DEPRECIATION
590 REMARK:   ( ACCUMULATED DEP. ) = ( OLD ACCUM. DEP. ) + ( DEP. )
600      LET       T       = (      T      ) + ( D   )
610 REMARK:   PRINTING OF TABLE
620       PRINT USING 140 , C , B , D , T , B1
630 REMARK:   END BOOK VAL OF PREVIOUS YR BECOMES BEG BOOK BAL OF NEW YR
640      LET B = B1
650 REMARK:   IF THE YRS COMPLETED < FINAL YR THEN CONTROL GOES TO 480
660      IF S < B THEN 480
680      END
```

Instructions for Using the SUMYEARS Program

Step 1. Sign onto the computer time-sharing system:

USER NUMBER, PASSWORD—

▨▨▨▨▨▨▨▨▨▨▨▨▨▨▨▨▨▨▨▨▨▨▨▨▨

Step 2. Run the SUMYEARS program to produce a sum-of-the-digits depreciation schedule. Enter the (1) cost, (2) salvage value, (3) estimated life in years, and (4) the name of the asset when asked by the program.

```
RUN SUMYEARS

SUMYEARS

SUM OF THE DIGITS (YEARS) DEPRECIATION METHOD

ENTER COST OF ASSET ? 6000
ENTER SALVAGE VALUE ?   500
ENTER NO. OF YEARS   ?    10
ENTER NAME OF ASSET (LESS THAN 16 CHARACTERS) ? MACHINE #3547


SUM OF THE DIGITS (YEARS) DEPRECIATION SCHEDULE FOR MACHINE #3547
```

YEAR	BOOK VALUE BEG. OF YR.	ANNUAL DEPRECIATION	ACCUMULATED DEPRECIATION	BOOK VALUE END OF YR.
1	6000.00	1000.00	1000.00	5000.00
2	5000.00	900.00	1900.00	4100.00
3	4100.00	800.00	2700.00	3300.00
4	3300.00	700.00	3400.00	2600.00
5	2600.00	600.00	4000.00	2000.00
6	2000.00	500.00	4500.00	1500.00
7	1500.00	400.00	4900.00	1100.00
8	1100.00	300.00	5200.00	800.00
9	800.00	200.00	5400.00	600.00
10	600.00	100.00	5500.00	500.00

```
PROCESSING     0 UNITS
```

DECLINING-BALANCE DEPRECIATION METHOD

The declining-balance depreciation method provides higher depreciation charges during the early years of a fixed asset's life. The method applies a constant depreciation rate to a decreasing book value. The result of applying this constant rate is a decreasing depreciation charge per period.

The declining-balance depreciation method allows depreciation charges between 100 and 200% of the straight-line depreciation rate on assets with an estimated life of three or more years.

Under the declining-balance depreciation method, the salvage value of an asset is not considered in the calculation of depreciation charges, but the ending book value can never be less than the estimated salvage value of the asset.

Calculating Declining-Balance Depreciation

The declining-balance depreciation procedure applies a constant-depreciation rate to a decreasing book value of an asset. The constant-depreciation rate is computed at a certain percentage of the straight-line rate. Therefore, the constant declining-balance depreciation rate is computed by (1) computing the straight-line rate, and (2) by multiplying this rate by a percentage value between 100 and 200% of the straight-line rate. The straight-line rate equals the cost of the asset divided by its estimated life divided again by the cost of the asset. The yearly declining-balance depreciation charges are then calculated by multiplying this constant declining-balance depreciation rate by the yearly beginning book values of the asset.

For example, using the 200%, or double, declining-balance method in determining a depreciation schedule on a machine costing $7,000, having an estimated salvage value of $600, and having an estimated life of five years, the constant depreciation rate would be computed as follows:

$$\frac{1}{\text{No. of years}} \times 200\% = \text{constant depreciation rate}$$

$$\frac{1}{5 \text{ (years)}} \times 2.0 = 0.4$$

The double declining-balance depreciation rate is then multiplied by each beginning year's book value to obtain the yearly depreciation charges, as illustrated in Table 8.4.

TABLE 8.4
CALCULATION OF DECLINE DEPRECIATION

Year	Book Value Beg. of Year, $	Annual Depreciation, $	Book Value End of Year, $
1	7,000.00	2,800.00	4,200.00
2	4,200.00	1,680.00	2,520.00
3	2,520.00	1,008.00	1,512.00
4	1,512.00	604.80	907.20
5	907.20	307.20	600.00

Notice in Table 8.4 that in the fifth year the actual annual depreciation charge is $362.88 (0.4 × 907.20), and the resulting ending book value would be $544.32 (907.20 − 362.88). Since this ending book value is $55.68 less than the estimated salvage value ($600), the depreciation charge in the fifth year ($362.88) was recalculated by decreasing it to $307.20, thus adjusting the difference between the beginning book value and the estimated salvage value of the asset. This modification of the schedule allows the ending book value in the fifth year to equal the salvage value of the asset.

The DECLINE Program

The DECLINE program creates a declining-balance depreciation schedule including (1) year number, (2) book value of the asset at the beginning of the year, (3) annual depreciation, (4) accumulated depreciation, and (5) book value of the asset at the end of the current year.

The DECLINE program also includes programming that allows for partial first- and last-year depreciation amortization. The following section includes a description, program flowchart (Fig. 8.4), and illustration of the DECLINE program.

THE DECLINE PROGRAM CASE STUDY

Purpose: The DECLINE program prepares a declining-balance depreciation schedule. Figure 8.4 shows the program flowchart. As before, Table 8.2, which lists variable names used in the program, also applies.

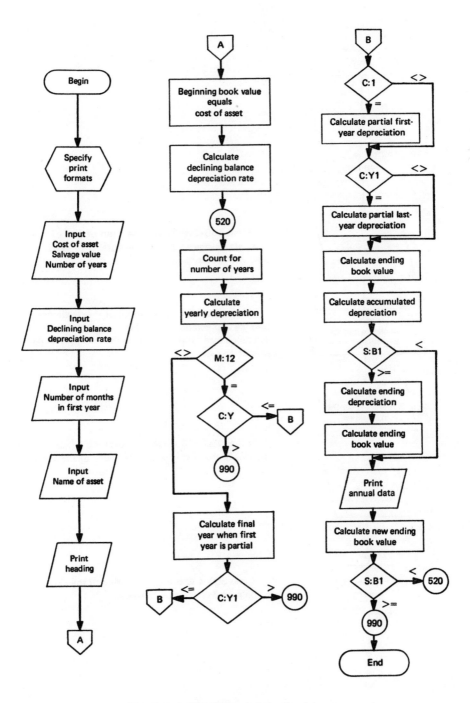

Fig. 8.4 DECLINE program flowchart.

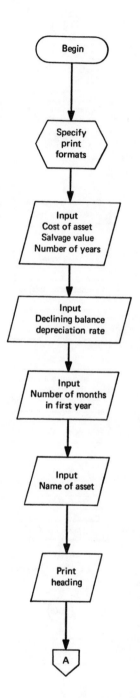

Lines 150–240 require the input of cost of the asset, its salvage value, and the number of years over which it is to be depreciated.

Lines 250–270 require input of the declining-balance depreciation rate. This depreciation rate can range from 100 to 200% of the straight-line depreciation rate.

Lines 280–340 require input of the number of months in the first year and the name of the asset.

Lines 350–430 print the heading of the declining-balance depreciation schedule.

138

```
100 REMARK:  SPECIFY THE PRINT FORMATS
110:DECLINING BALANCE DEPRECIATION SCHEDULE FOR ###############
120:          BOOK VALUE      ANNUAL          ACCUMULATED      BOOK VALUE
130:YEAR      BEG. OF YR.     DEPRECIATION    DEPRECIATION     END OF YR.
140: ##       ########.##     #########.##    #########.##     #######.##
150 REMARK:  INPUT COST OF ASSET (A), SALVAGE VALUE (S),
160 REMARK:  AND NUMBER OF YEARS (Y)
170          PRINT 'DECLINING BALANCE DEPRECIATION METHOD'
180          PRINT
190          PRINT 'ENTER COST OF ASSET ';
200          INPUT A
210          PRINT 'ENTER SALVAGE VALUE ';
220          INPUT S
230          PRINT 'ENTER NO. OF YEARS   ';
240          INPUT Y
250 REMARK:  INPUT DECLINING BALANCE DEPRECIATION RATE.
260          PRINT 'ENTER DEPRECIATION RATE IN PERCENT';
270          INPUT P
280 REMARK:  NO. OF MONTHS IN FIRST YEAR (M),
290 REMARK:  AND THE NAME OF THE ASSET (N$).
300          PRINT 'IN FIRST YEAR'
310          PRINT 'ENTER NO. OF MONTHS ';
320          INPUT M
330          PRINT 'ENTER NAME OF ASSET (LESS THAN 16 CHARACTERS) ';
340          INPUT N$
350 REMARK:  PRINTING OF HEADING
360          PRINT
370          PRINT
380          PRINT
390          PRINT USING 110, N$
400          PRINT
410          PRINT USING 120
420          PRINT USING 130
430          PRINT
```

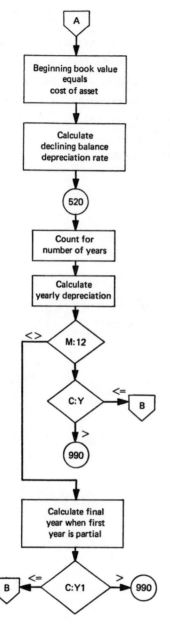

Lines 440–450 set the beginning book value of the asset equal to the cost of the asset.

Lines 490–510 calculate the declining-balance depreciation rate: The rate equals a percentage of the declining-balance depreciation rates multiplied by the conversion factor (0.01), multiplied by the straight-line rate determined in line 480.

Lines 540–560 calculate the yearly declining-balance depreciation for the asset: The amount of depreciation equals the rate determined in line 510 multiplied by the book value of the asset.

Lines 570–590 test for a partial first year.

Lines 600–610 test to find if the number of the current year is less than, or equal to, the total number of years over which the asset is to be depreciated.

Lines 640–650 (y1) equal the final year plus 1 if the first year is partial.

Lines 660–670 test to determine if the number of the current year is less than, or equal to, the number of the years over which the asset is to be depreciated.

140

```
440 REMARK:  SET BEGINNING BOOK VALUE EQUAL TO COST OF ASSET.

450     B = A

500 REMARK: RATE = ST LINE RATE *  PERCENTAGE

510     LET  R = ( 1/Y )     * ( P/100 )

520 REMARK:  VARIABLE (C) IS USED AS A COUNTER FOR THE NUMBER OF YRS.

530     C = C + 1

540 REMARK:  CALCULATE YEARLY DEPRECIATION.

550 REMARK:  ( DEPRECIATION ) = ( RATE ) * ( BOOK VALUE )

560     LET      D        = ( R ) * (     B     )

570 REMARK:  TEST FOR PARTIAL FIRST YEAR.

590     IF M <> 12 THEN 650

600 REMARK:  CONTROL TRANSFERRED TO 710 IF NO. OF YRS. <= FINAL YR.

610     IF C <=  Y THEN 710

630     GO TO 990

640 REMARK:  (Y1) EQUALS THE FINAL YR. IF 1ST. YR. IS PARTIAL.

650     Y1 = Y + 1

660 REMARK:  IF SCHEDULE IS NOT FINISHED THEN CONTROL IS TRANS. TO 710.

670     IF C <= Y1 THEN 710

690     GO TO 990
```

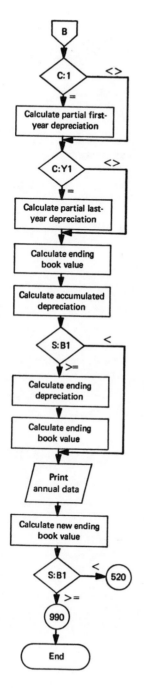

Lines 700–710 calculate the partial first-year depreciation.

Lines 750–760 test to find if the current year is not equal to the final year. If it is not, control is transferred to line 820.

Lines 770–790 calculate the partial last-year depreciation: The depreciation equals 1 minus the number of months in the first year divided by 12 months and multiplied by the yearly depreciation rate.

Lines 830–840 calculate accumulated depreciation.

Lines 850–860 test to determine if the salvage value of the asset is less than the ending balance of the current year. If it is, control is transferred to line 930.

Line 870–890 calculate the depreciation when the yearly depreciation is greater than, or equal to, the ending book value of the asset. Depreciation equals the beginning book value of the asset minus its salvage value.

Lines 900–910 calculate the ending book value of the asset. Ending book value equals salvage value of the asset.

Lines 920–930 print the straight-line depreciation annual data.

Lines 940–950 set the beginning book value of the new year equal to the ending book value of the preceding year.

Lines 960–970 test to find if the ending book value is less than the salvage value of the asset. If it is, control is transferred to line 520.

Line 990 ends the program.

142

```
700 REMARK:  IF THE COUNTER <> 1ST. YR. THEN CONTROL IS TRANS. TO 760.
710      IF C <> 1 THEN 760
720 REMARK:  CALCULATION OF PARTIAL FIRST YEAR DEPRECIATION
730 REMARK:  ( 1 ST. YR. DEP. ) = ( NO. OF MTHS. / 12 ) * ( YRLY DEP. )
740      LET       D       = (    M       / 12.) * (     D     )
750 REMARK:  IF COUNTER <> FINAL YR. THEN CONTROL IS TRANS. TO 820.
760      IF C <> Y1 THEN 820
770 REMARK:  CALCULATION OF PARTIAL LAST YR. DEPRECIATION
780 REMARK:  ( DEP. ) = ( 1 - ( MTHS. / 12. ) ) * ( YRLY DEP. )
790      LET   D   = ( 1 - ( M    / 12. ) ) * (     D     )
800 REMARK:  CALCULATION OF YRLY ENDING BOOK VALUE
810 REMARK:  ( ENDING BOOK VAL. ) = ( BEG. BK. VAL. ) - ( DEPRECIATION
820      LET       B1       = (     B     ) - (     D
830 REMARK:  ( ACCUMULATED DEP. ) = ( OLD ACCUM. DEP. ) + ( DEP. )
840      LET       T       = (       T     ) + ( D  )
850  REMARK: IF SAL. VAL. < END. BAL. THEN CONTROL IS TRANS. TO 930
860      IF S < B1 THEN 930
870 REMARK:  CALCULATION OF DEP. WHEN YRLY DEP. >= END. BOOK VALUE.
880 REMARK:  ( DEPRECIATION ) = ( BEG. BOOK VALUE ) - ( SALVAGE VALUE )
890      LET       D       = (     B     ) - (     S     )
900 REMARK:  ( ENDING BOOK VALUE ) = ( SALVAGE VALUE )
910      LET       B1       ' = (     S     )
920 REMARK:  PRINTING OF TABLE
930      PRINT USING 140, C, B, D, T, B1
940 REMARK:  END BOOK VAL OF PREVIOUS YR BECOMES BEG BOOK VAL OF NEW YR
950      B = B1
960 REMARK:  IF SAL. VAL. < ENDING BK VAL THEN CONTROL IS TRAN TO 520
970      IF S < B1 THEN 520
990      END
```

Instructions for Using the DECLINE Program

Step 1. Sign onto the computer time-sharing system:

USER NUMBER, PASSWORD—

▨▨▨▨▨▨▨▨▨▨▨▨▨▨▨▨▨▨▨▨▨▨▨▨▨

Step 2. Run the DECLINE program to produce a declining-balance depreciation schedule. Enter the (1) cost, (2) salvage value, (3) estimated life, (4) depreciation rate in percent, (5) number of months in the first year over which the asset will be depreciated, and (6) name of the asset. The depreciation rate is generally 200%, but any rate between 100 and 200% may be used.

```
RUN

DECLINE


DECLINING BALANCE DEPRECIATION METHOD


ENTER COST OF ASSET ?  10000.00

ENTER SALVAGE VALUE ?   1500.00

ENTER NO. OF YEARS   ?      6

ENTER DEPRECIATION RATE IN PERCENT?  200

IN FIRST YEAR

ENTER NO. OF MONTHS ?  12

ENTER NAME OF ASSET (LESS THAN 16 CHARACTERS) ? MACHINE #7944



DECLINING BALANCE DEPRECIATION SCHEDULE FOR MACHINE #7944
```

YEAR	BOOK VALUE BEG. OF YR.	ANNUAL DEPRECIATION	ACCUMULATED DEPRECIATION	BOOK VALUE END OF YR.
1	10000.00	3333.33	3333.33	6666.66
2	6666.66	2222.22	5555.55	4444.44
3	4444.44	1481.48	7037.03	2962.96
4	2962.96	987.65	8024.68	1975.31
5	1975.31	475.31	8683.11	1500.00

```
PROCESSING      1 UNITS
```

UNITS-OF-PRODUCTION DEPRECIATION METHOD

We have mentioned that depreciation results both from use and through passage of time. The units-of-production method of depreciation reflects a product's use; that is, it reflects the physical wear and tear on an asset. For example, if a machine cost $22,000, had a $1,000 salvage value, and produced 40,000 parts the first year, 5,000 parts the second year, 60,000 parts the third year, and no parts in the fourth year, none of the depreciation methods relating to time could provide an equitable depreciation charge for all four periods. Therefore, we use the units-of-production depreciation method to allocate depreciation charges when the use of fixed assets varies greatly from year to year.

Calculating Units-of-Production Depreciation

To calculate a units-of-production depreciation schedule, calculate the rate of depreciation per unit. Subtract the salvage value from the cost of the asset and divide the result by the total number of units the asset is estimated to produce. Then multiply the rate of depreciation per unit by the number of units produced in any particular accounting period. This yields the depreciation charge for that period.

Using the example mentioned above, calculate the depreciation rate per unit of production as follows:

$$\frac{\text{Cost} - \text{salvage value}}{\text{Total units}} = \frac{\$22,000 - \$1,000}{105,000} = \$0.20 \text{ per unit}$$

Multiply the depreciation rate per unit by the number of units produced each year. This yields the depreciation schedule given in Table 8.5.

The units-of-production depreciation method can be used to allocate depreciation according to any measure of use. Often it is used for miles driven or hours of use.

TABLE 8.5
THE UNITS DEPRECIATION SCHEDULE

Year	Book Value Beg. of Year, $	Units	Annual Depreciation, $	Book Value End of Year, $
1	22,000	40,000	8,000	14,000
2	14,000	5,000	1,000	13,000
3	13,000	60,000	12,000	1,000
4	1,000	0	0	1,000

The UNITS Program

The UNITS program creates a units-of-production depreciation schedule for fixed assets whose use varies greatly from year to year. The depreciation schedule includes (1) year number, (2) book value of the asset at the beginning of the year, (3) annual depreciation charge, (4) units produced in the current year, (5) total units produced over the life of the asset, and (6) the book value of the asset at the end of the year.

This section includes a description, program flowchart, and illustration of the UNITS program.

THE UNITS PROGRAM CASE STUDY

Purpose: The UNITS program prepares a units-of-production depreciation schedule. Figure 8.5 presents the program flowchart. Again refer to Table 8.2 for the variable names used in the program.

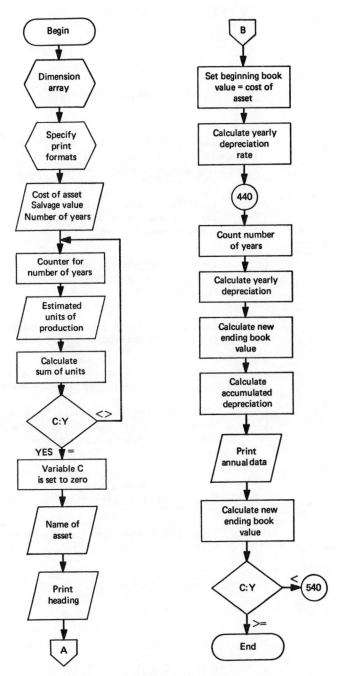

Fig. 8.5 UNITS program flowchart.

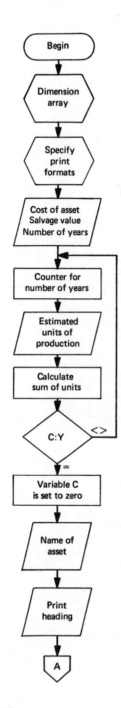

Line 100 dimensions the variable U.

Lines 110–150 are the image statements that specify the print formats for the units-of-production depreciation schedule program.

Lines 160–250 require the input of the cost of the asset, the salvage value, and the number of years the asset is to be depreciated.

Lines 260–270 state that the variable C is used as a counter for the number of years of the depreciation schedule.

Lines 280–310 require the estimated unit production per year in the depreciation schedule.

Lines 320–330 sum the estimated total units produced during the depreciated life of the asset.

Lines 340–350 test to determine if the number of years entered is less than the final year of the depreciated life of the asset. If so, the control is transferred to line 270.

Lines 360–370 set C equal to 0. This statement allows the variable C to be used as the counter for the number of years completed in the table.

Lines 380–390 require the input of the name of the asset.

```
100        DIM U(50)
110 REMARK:  SPECIFY THE PRINT FORMATS
120:UNITS OF PRODUCTION DEPRECIATION SCHEDULE FOR ###############
130:         BOOK VALUE      ANNUAL                      BOOK VALUE
140:YEAR     BEG. OF YR.     DEPRECIATION      UNITS     END OF YR.
150: ##      ########.##     #########.## ###### OF ######  #######.##
160 REMARK:  INPUT COST OF ASSET (A), SALVAGE VALUE (S),
170 REMARK:  AND NUMBER OF YEARS (Y)
180        PRINT 'UNITS OF PRODUCTION METHOD'
190        PRINT
200        PRINT 'ENTER COST OF ASSET ';
210        INPUT A
220        PRINT 'ENTER SALVAGE VALUE ';
230        INPUT S
240        PRINT 'ENTER NO. OF YEARS   ';
250        INPUT Y
255        PRINT 'ENTER ESTIMATED UNITS OF PRODUCTION'
260 REMARK:  VARIABLE C IS A COUNTER FOR YEARS
270        LET C = C + 1
280 REMARK:  ENTER ESTIMATED UNIT PRODUCTION FOR EACH YEAR
300        PRINT 'FOR YR. NUMBER'C;
310        INPUT U(C)
320 REMARK:  VARIABLE X IS A SUMMER FOR ESTIMATED TOTAL UNITS PRODUCED
330        LET X = X + U(C)
340 REMARK:  IF # OF YRS < FINAL YR THEN CONTROL IS TRANSFERRED TO 270
350        IF C < Y THEN 270
360 REMARK:  VARIABLE C IS SET TO ZERO
370        LET C = 0
380        PRINT 'ENTER NAME OF ASSET (LESS THAN 16 CHARACTERS) ';
390        INPUT N$
```

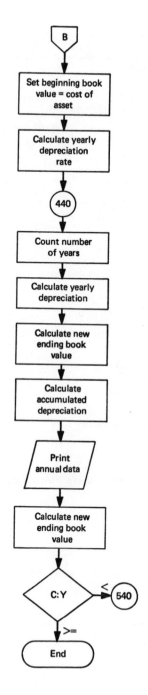

Lines 400–470 print the heading of the units-of-production depreciation schedule.

Lines 480–490 set the beginning book value of the asset equal to the cost of the asset.

Lines 500–520 calculate the depreciation rate per unit of production: Depreciation equals the cost of the asset minus its salvage value divided by the total number of units produced by the asset.

Lines 530–540 count the number of years over which the asset will be depreciated.

Lines 550–570 calculate the yearly depreciation: Yearly depreciation equals the depreciation rate calculated in line 520 times the number of the current year.

Lines 580–600 calculate the yearly ending book value: Ending book value equals the value at the beginning of the current year minus the depreciation incurred that year.

Lines 610–620 calculate the accumulated depreciation where accumulative depreciation equals the previously accumulated depreciation plus the current year's depreciation.

Lines 630–640 print the units of production depreciation data.

Lines 650–660 set the beginning book value of the new year equal to the ending book value of the previous year.

Lines 670–680 test to verify if the number of the current year is less than that of the final year of the depreciation schedule. If so, control is transferred to line 440.

Line 690 ends the program.

150

```
400 REMARK:  PRINTING OF HEADING
410       PRINT
420       PRINT
430       PRINT USING 120, N$
440       PRINT
450       PRINT USING 130
460       PRINT USING 140
470       PRINT
480 REMARK:  SET BEGINNING BOOK VALUE EQUAL TO COST OF ASSET.
490       B = A
500 REMARK:  CALCULATION OF DEPRECIATION RATE PER UNIT
510 REMARK:  RATE = ( ASSET - SALVAGE VALUE ) / ( TOTAL UNITS )
520       LET R   = (    A    -    S    ) / (    X    )
530 REMARK:  VARIABLE (C) IS USED AS A COUNTER FOR THE NUMBER OF YEARS
540       C = C + 1
550 REMARK:  CALCULATION OF YRLY DEPRECIATION
560 REMARK:  DEPRECIATION = ( RATE ) * ( EST. YRLY PRODUCTION )
570       LET    D    = (  R  ) * (      U(C)      )
580 REMARK:  CALCULATION OF YRLY ENDING BOOK VALUE
590 REMARK:  ( END BOOK VAL ) = ( BEG BOOK VALUE ) - ( DEPRECIATION )
600       LET    B1    = (     B     ) - (    D    )
610 REMARK:  ( ACCUMULATED DEP. ) = ( OLD ACCUM. DEP. ) + ( DEP. )
620       LET    T        = (     T     ) + ( D )
630 REMARK:  PRINTING OF TABLE
640       PRINT USING 150, C, B, D, U(C), X, B1
650 REMARK:  END BOOK VAL OF PREVIOUS YR BECOMES BEG BOOK VAL OF NEW YR
660       B = B1
670 REMARK:  IF COUNTER < FINAL YR THEN CONTROL IS TRANSFERRED TO 540
680       IF    C   <      Y  THEN   540
690 END
```

Instructions for Using the UNITS Program

Step 1. Sign onto the computer time-sharing system:

USER NUMBER, PASSWORD–

██ ██ ██ ██ ██ ██ ██ ██ ██ ██ ██ ██ ██ ██ ██ ██ ██ ██

Step 2. Run the UNITS program to produce a units of production depreciation schedule. Enter the (1) cost, (2) salvage value, (3) estimated life in years, and (4) estimated units of production per year.

```
RUN UNITS

UNITS

UNITS OF PRODUCTION METHOD

ENTER COST OF ASSET ? 17000
ENTER SALVAGE VALUE ?  1000
ENTER NO. OF YEARS   ?     4
ENTER ESTIMATED UNITS OF PRODUCTION
FOR YR. NUMBER 1     ?  1250
FOR YR. NUMBER 2     ?  2000
FOR YR. NUMBER 3     ?  3250
FOR YR. NUMBER 4     ?  1500
ENTER NAME OF ASSET (LESS THAN 16 CHARACTERS) ? MACHINE #450


UNITS OF PRODUCTION DEPRECIATION SCHEDULE FOR MACHINE #450

              BOOK VALUE     ANNUAL                         BOOK VALUE
    YEAR      BEG. OF YR.    DEPRECIATION      UNITS         END OF YR.

      1        17000.00        2500.00     1250 OF  8000      14500.00
      2        14500.00        4000.00     2000 OF  8000      10500.00
      3        10500.00        6500.00     3250 OF  8000       4000.00
      4         4000.00        3000.00     1500 OF  8000       1000.00

    PROCESSING       0 UNITS
```

QUESTIONS

1. What are the primary causes of depreciation?
2. Physical wear and tear of an asset is often the result of asset's use. What depreciation method best reflects an asset's use?
3. Technological obsolescence, caused by new inventions and technical improvements, is related to the passage of time. What depreciation methods best reflect the passage of time?
4. What information is necessary to compute a straight-line depreciation schedule?
5. What factors are included in the cost of a fixed asset?
6. When is the sum-of-the-digits depreciation method used?

7. Does the sum-of-the-year's digits method provide an increasing or decreasing depreciation charge per period?
8. When is the units-of-production depreciation method used?
9. Currently, which depreciation method is most widely used? Why?
10. What is the main disadvantage of the straight-line depreciation method?
11. When does the straight-line depreciation method provide an equitable allocation of total depreciation charges?
12. How is the straight-line depreciation calculated?
13. What depreciation method provides higher depreciation charges during the early years of the life of a fixed asset by applying a constant depreciation rate to its decreasing book value?
14. How is salvage value of an asset considered in the calculation of the declining-balance depreciation charge?

PROBLEMS

1. On January 1 the Del Ray Corporation purchased a machine, No. 75305, for $27,000. The company estimates that the machine will have a life of ten years, with a salvage value of $4,000. Maintenance and repair charges will be minimal during the first few years of service, but the charges will increase as the asset grows older. Determine the depreciation method that would provide the most equitable depreciation allocation, and create a 15-year depreciation schedule for the asset.

2. The Raow Company purchased a 7505 lathe for $2,450 on June 1. The lathe has an estimated life of ten years and an estimated salvage value of $400. What is the depreciation charge on the asset for the remainder of the first year if the straight-line depreciation method is used? Create a straight-line depreciation schedule for the 7505 lathe.

3. The Johnson Printing Company purchased a new printing press for $3,700 on January 1, 19___. The printing press has an estimated life of seven years and a salvage value of $450. The owner estimates that the press will have about the same use for all seven years, but maintenance charges will increase as the asset grows older. Determine which depreciation method would allow the greatest depreciation charges in the first three years, and create a seven-year depreciation schedule for the printing press.

4. Alcon Manufacturing Company purchased a molding machine for $13,000. It has an estimated life of five years and an estimated salvage value of $790. The machine is scheduled to produce the following parts:

Year	Estimated Production
1	3,600
2	1,000
3	3,800
4	1,500
5	1,200
Total	11,100

Determine which depreciation method would produce the most equitable depreciation charges for each period. Create a five-year depreciation schedule for the machine.

9

CREATING A COMPUTERIZED
ACCOUNTING SYSTEM

Chapters 1–3 introduced concepts of data processing systems, flowcharting, and elements of the BASIC programming language. Chapters 4–8 applied these concepts to accounting systems, including the General Ledger, Income Statement, Balance Sheet, Accounts Receivable, Payroll Register, and the Depreciation Schedule.

An accountant not only must understand the various concepts of accounting systems, but also must be able to integrate these concepts into a computerized accounting system. The purpose of this chapter is to provide a case study of a company that requires the following reports:

1. General Ledger.
2. Income Statement.
3. Balance Sheet.
4. Accounts Receivable Ledger.
5. Payroll Register.
6. Depreciation Schedules.

THE TAPESTRY PHOTO CASE STUDY

Objective. To create a Chart of Accounts for the Tapestry Photo Company.

Background. On January 1, Tom Bauer invested $10,000 to begin a small industrial photography company. He rented a furnished studio for $500 a month, paid a month's utilities expense of $15, and purchased $30 of office supplies for January. Mr. Bauer then bought an industrial camera with an estimated life of ten years, which cost $2,000 and had a salvage value of $500. He hired four photographers: Ted Baxter, Ralph Conley, Gary Johnson, and Dave Williams. Each photographer furnished his own camera equipment.

Tapestry Photo operated for three weeks without a formalized accounting system, but when Mr. Bauer found that he couldn't determine his financial position, he decided to adopt a computerized accounting system. Your task is to create a computerized accounting system for the Tapestry Photo Company, including the following:

1. Payroll Register.
2. Depreciation Schedule.
3. Accounts Receivable Ledger.
4. General Ledger.
5. Income Statement.
6. Balance Sheet.

The payroll information for all workers for the first three weeks of January is listed in Table 9.1. All five men worked 40 hours during the fourth week.

TABLE 9.1
TAPESTRY PHOTO PAYROLL

Employee No. and Name		Tax Ded.	Hourly Wage, $	Year-to-date Totals		
				Gross, $	FIT, $	FICA, $
1	Tom Bauer	2	10.00	1200.00	182.27	61.25
2	Ted Baxter	1	5.50	660.00	132.00	33.15
3	Ralph Conley	2	5.50	660.00	121.00	33.15
4	Gary Johnson	1	5.50	660.00	132.00	33.15
5	Dave Williams	3	5.50	660.00	110.00	33.15

TABLE 9.2
TAPESTRY PHOTO ACCOUNTS RECEIVABLE

Date	Invoice	Customer No.	Customer Name	Charges, $	Payments, $
1/2	1000	100	Lakewood Realty	160.00	
1/6	1001	110	Aspen Motors	960.00	
1/6	1002	120	Chambers & Sons	500.00	
1/10	1003	130	Frohlick Const.	1800.00	
1/18	1004	140	Western Roofing	1408.00	
1/6	1002	120	Chambers & Sons		500.00
1/22	1005	150	Town & Country, Inc.	1800.00	
1/2	1000	100	Lakewood Realty		160.00
1/10	1003	130	Frohlick Constr.		1800.00
1/25	1006	160	Art Master	200.00	
1/30	1007	170	Sav-U-Mor	116.17	
1/18	1004	140	Western Roofing		1200.00
1/22	1005	150	Town & Country Inc.		1800.00

Mr. Bauer wants a straight-line depreciation schedule for his industrial camera equipment, and he wants to account for depreciation only at the close of the year.

Tapestry Photo's accounts receivable for January are given in Table 9.2. Note that the end of the fourth week in January was also the end of the month. This eliminates the need to include an additional partial week.

PROCEDURE

Create a Payroll Register for the Tapestry Photo Company

1. Make an origin-data file for the payroll system, including line number, employee number, employee name, number of payroll deductions, hourly wage, and year-to-date gross pay.

2. Run the CREATE program to create your payroll master file from the origin file. This program reads the origin-data file and creates the payroll master file.

3. Run the ADJUST program to list the employee master file. Use this list to verify data entered. If incorrect, make the necessary change in your origin file, SAVE it and perform Step 6 again, and continue on.

4. Create the current week's HOURS file for the fourth week by running the HOURS program. Enter a line number and a zero (e.g., 999 0) after the last employee's hour has been entered.

5. Run the PAY program to calculate and print the Payroll Register and update the payroll master file.

Since the year-to-date totals are the totals for January, the year-to-date gross pay, FIT and FICA, and net pay values will later be entered in the General Ledger transactions file.

Run the STLINE program to create a straight-line depreciation schedule for the industrial camera. Depreciation is posted to the General Ledger at the end of the year.

Produce an Aged Accounts Receivable Ledger

1. Make an origin file for the Accounts Receivable system. Each record in this file should contain line number, customer number, customer name, and number of outstanding invoices.

Since all accounts are new accounts, the number of outstanding invoices equals zero for each account. The names and customer numbers for the beginning balance file can be determined from the list of accounts receivable for January.

2. Run the ARCREATE program to create your individual Accounts Receivable Ledger file. Be sure to initialize your Accounts Receivable file before running the ARCREATE program.

3. Make an Accounts Receivable transactions file, including line number, customer number, invoice number, invoice date (month, number, day), and the amount of the invoice.

New invoices are entered with a positive amount figure; payments are entered with a negative amount figure. Enter a record of 999 999, 9, 9, 9, 9 after the last transaction.

4. Run the ARPOST program to post your transactions to the Accounts Receivable master file. Totals of payments, new invoices, and accounts receivable will later be posted to the General Ledger transactions file.

5. Run the AGEREPT program to print the Aged Accounts Receivable report. Enter the month number for January (1), December (12), and November (11) as the dates for the aging categories.

Produce a General Ledger for the Tapestry Photo Company.

Required:

1. Make an origin file for the General Ledger, including line number, account number, account name, and beginning balances for each record. Make the following four entries:

(a) Following the asset accounts, enter record line number 1, ASSETS, 0
(b) Following the liability accounts, enter record line number 2, LIABILITIES, 0
(c) Following the income accounts, enter the record line number 3, INCOME, 0
(d) Following the expense accounts, enter record line number 4, EXPENSE, 0

Debit the cash account with $10,000 and credit the owner's equity account with −10,000. All other accounts should have beginning balances of zero. The last line in the file should be

line number 999, 'END', 9

Be sure to save the beginning balances file.

2. Run the GLCREATE program to create your individual General Ledger file. Be sure to initialize your General Ledger file name before running the GLCREATE program.

3. Make a General Ledger transactions file for January. At least two entries must be made for each transaction: one to the debit account and one to the credit account. Each entry consists of line number, account number,

description, transaction reference number, and amount (the amount is negative for credit entries). The final line must include the following:

line number 999, 0, 0

The transactions include:

(a) Payment of rent.
(b) Payment of utilities.
(c) Purchase of office supplies.
(d) Purchase of industrial camera.
(e) Payroll, including payroll expense, cash payment of net pay, FIT payable, and FICA payable.
(f) January invoices, including revenue, cash, and accounts receivable.
(g) Purchase of film.

APPENDIXES
PROGRAMS AND ORIGIN DATA FILES

A. TRIBAL
B. INCSTMT
C. BALSHEET
D. AGEREPT
E. PAY
F. STLINE
G. SUMYEARS
H. DECLINE
I. UNITS
J. BEGBAL
K. GLCREATE
L. GLEDIT
M. ARBEGIN
N. ARCREATE
O. ARPOST
P. ARCHANGE
Q. CREATE
R. PAY1
S. ADJUST
T. HOURS

160

APPENDIX A

```
                    TRIBAL

GENERAL LEDGER SYSTEM

  1 REMARK: SPECIFY THE TRIAL BALANCE PRINT FORMATS
  2:###################     GENERAL LEDGER TRIAL BALANCE     ##################
  3:ACCOUNT      ACCOUNT                                                ACCOUNT
  4:NUMBER        NAME           REFERENCE      DEBIT       CREDIT      BALANCE
  5: ###     ###################          BEGINNING BALANCE            #####.##
  6:              ###################     #####    ######.##
  7:              ###################     #####              ######.##
  8:                                        ENDING BALANCE              #####.##
  9:          TRIAL BALANCE                 ######.##   ######.##   #####.##
 10  REMARK:  SPECIFY ARRAY SIZES
 20        DIM A(50), N$(50), B(50), E(100), D$(100), R(100), V(100)
100 REMARK: INPUT FILE NAMES, COMPANY NAME, & DATE
110       PRINT 'ENTER GENERAL LEDGER MASTER & TRANSACTION FILE NAMES ';
120       INPUT G$,T$
130       PRINT 'ENTER COMPANY NAME ,   REPORT DATE ';
140       INPUT C$,Y$
160 REMARK: ATTACH FILES TO THE PROGRAM
170       OPEN 1, G$, INPUT
180       OPEN 2, T$, INPUT
190 REMARK: READ TRANSACTION FILE
200       LET I = I + 1
210       GET 2: E(I), D$(I), R(I), V(I)
220       IF E(I) = 999 GOTO 250
240       GOTO 200
250       LET I = I - 1
260 REMARK: PRINT HEADINGS FOR GENERAL LEDGER TRIAL BALANCE REPORT
270       PRINT
280       PRINT USING 2, C$, Y$
290       PRINT
300       PRINT USING 3
310       PRINT USING 4
320       PRINT
330 REMARK: READ ACCOUNT BEGINNING BALANCE FROM GENERAL LEDGER FILE
340       LET J = J + 1
350       GET 1: A(J), N$(J), B(J)
360       IF A(J) < 100 GOTO 340
370       IF A(J) = 999 GOTO 650
380 REMARK: PRINT ACCOUNT BEGINNING BALANCE
390       PRINT USING 5, A(J), N$(J), B(J)
400 REMARK: CHECK FOR TRANSACTIONS THAT APPLY TO "THIS" GL ACCOUNT
410       LET K = K + 1
420       IF E(K) = A(J) GOTO 460
440       IF K <= I GOTO 410
450       GOTO 580
460 REMARK: IF TRANSACTION AMOUNT IS NEGATIVE, IT IS A CREDIT
470       IF V(K) < 0 GOTO 530
480 RFMARK: PRINT AND TOTAL DEBIT TRANSACTIONS
490       PRINT USING 6, D$(K), R(K), V(K)
500       LET T1 = T1 + V(K)
510       GOTO 550
520 REMARK: PRINT AND TOTAL CREDIT TRANSACTIONS
530       PRINT USING 7, D$(K), R(K), V(K)
540       LET T2 = T2 + V(K)
550 REMARK: POST TRANSACTION AMOUNT TO ACCOUNT BALANCE
560       LET B(J) = B(J) + V(K)
570       GOTO 410
580 REMARK: PRINT ENDING ACCOUNT BALANCE
590       PRINT USING 8, B(J)
```

GENERAL LEDGER SYSTEM

```
600        PRINT
610 REMARK: TOTAL ENDING BALANCES OF ACCOUNTS (TRIAL BALANCE)
620        LET T9 = T9 + B(J)
630        LET K = 0
640        GOTO 340
650 REMARK: PRINT TRIAL BALANCE
660        PRINT
670        PRINT USING 9, T1, T2, T9
680        PRINT
690        PRINT
700 REMARK: DETERMINE IF MASTER FILE SHOULD BE UPDATED
710        PRINT 'DO YOU WISH TO UPDATE THE  GENERAL LEDGER FILE NOW ';
720        INPUT X$
730        IF X$ = 'NO' GOTO 820
735        IF X$ <> 'YES' GOTO 710
740 REMARK: STORE NEW GENERAL LEDGER RECORDS IN THE MASTER FILE
745        LET J = 0
750        OPEN 1, G$, OUTPUT
760        LET J = J + 1
770        PUT 1: A(J),.N$(J), B(J)
780        IF A(J) = 999 GOTO 820
800        GOTO 760
820 END
```

TOTAL PROGRAM LINES   81

APPENDIX B

INCSTMT

FINANCIAL STATEMENTS

```
  1 REMARK: SPECIFY THE INCOME STATEMENT PRINT FORMATS
  2:                      ####################
  3:                         INCOME STATEMENT        ####################
  4:   ACCOUNT NAME              ACCOUNT BALANCE
  5:###################          #####.##
  6:####################                             ######.##
  7:                                                 ==========
100 REMARK: INPUT FILE NAME, COMPANY NAME, REPORT DATE
110        PRINT 'ENTER YOUR GENERAL LEDGER FILE NAME';
120        INPUT G$
130        PRINT 'ENTER COMPANY NAME, REPORT DATE';
140        INPUT C$,D$
150 REMARK: ATTACH GENERAL LEDGER FILE TO THE PROGRAM
160        OPEN 1, G$, INPUT
170 REMARK: PRINT INCOME STATEMENT HEADINGS
180        PRINT
190        PRINT USING 2, C$
200        PRINT USING 3, D$
210        PRINT
220        PRINT USING 4
230        PRINT
240        PRINT 'INCOME'
250        PRINT
260 REMARK: READ ACCOUNT FROM GENERAL LEDGER FILE
270        GET 1: A, N$, B
280        IF A = 999 GOTO 540
290 REMARK: DETERMINE IF ALL INCOME OR EXPENSES HAVE PRINTED
300        IF A = 4 GOTO 410
```

FINANCIAL STATEMENTS

```
310        IF A = 5 GOTO 510
320 REMARK: SELECT INCOME AND EXPENSE ACCOUNTS
330        IF A < 400 GOTO 270
340 REMARK: DETERMINE IF ACCOUNT IS AN EXPENSE
350        IF A >= 500 GOTO 470
360 REMARK: SET BALANCE TO POSITIVE, TOTAL AND PRINT INCOME ACCTS
370        LET B = B * (-1)
380        LET I1 = I1 + B
390        PRINT USING 5, N$, B
400        GOTO 270
410 REMARK: PRINT TOTAL INCOME
420        PRINT USING 6, 'TOTAL INCOME', I1
430        PRINT
440        PRINT 'EXPENSES'
450        PRINT
460        GOTO 270
470 REMARK: TOTAL AND PRINT EXPENSE ACCTS
480        LET E1 = E1 + B
490        PRINT USING 5, N$, B
500        GOTO 270
510 REMARK: PRINT TOTAL EXPENSES
520        PRINT USING 6, 'TOTAL EXPENSE', E1
530        GOTO 270
540 REMARK: CALCULATE AND PRINT NET INCOME
550        LET N1 = I1 - E1
560        PRINT
570        PRINT USING 6, 'NET INCOME', N1
580        PRINT USING 7
600 END
```

TOTAL PROGRAM LINES   57

APPENDIX C

BALSHEET

FINANCIAL STATEMENTS

```
  1 REMARK: SPECIFY THE BALANCE SHEET PRINT FORMATS
  2:                        ##################
  3:                           BALANCE SHEET              ##################
  4:    ACCOUNT NAME              ACCOUNT BALANCE
  5:##################              ######.##
  6:##################                                    ######.##
  7:                                                      =========
100 REMARK: INPUT FILE NAME, COMPANY NAME, REPORT DATE, NET INCOME
110        PRINT 'ENTER YOUR GENERAL LEDGER FILE NAME   ';
120        INPUT G$
130        PRINT 'ENTER COMPANY NAME, REPORT DATE';
140        INPUT C$,D$
150        PRINT 'ENTER NET INCOME FROM INCOME STATEMENT';
160        INPUT N1
170 REMARK: ATTACH GENERAL LEDGER FILE NAME TO PROGRAM
180        OPEN 1, G$, INPUT
190 REMARK: PRINT BALANCE SHEET HEADINGS
200        PRINT
210        PRINT USING 2,C$
220        PRINT USING 3,D$
230        PRINT
240        PRINT USING 4
```

163

FINANCIAL STATEMENTS

```
250        PRINT
260        PRINT 'ASSETS'
270        PRINT
280 REMARK: READ ACCOUNT FROM GENERAL LEDGER FILE
290        GET 1: A, N$, B
300 REMARK: DETERMINE IF ALL ASSETS, LIAB OR CAPITAL HAVE PRINTED
310        IF A = 1 GOTO 420
320        IF A = 2 GOTO 570
330        IF A = 3 GOTO 650
340 REMARK: SELECT BALANCE SHEET ACCOUNTS
350        IF A >= 400 GOTO 700
360 REMARK: DETERMINE IF ACCOUNT IS LIAB. OR CAPITAL
370        IF A >= 200 GOTO 490
380 REMARK: TOTAL AND PRINT ASSETS
390        LET A1 = A1 + B
400        PRINT USING 5, N$, B
410        GOTO 290
420 REMARK: PRINT TOTAL ASSETS
430        PRINT USING 6, 'TOTAL ASSETS', A1
440        PRINT USING 7
450        PRINT
460        PRINT 'LIABILITIES & CAPITAL'
470        PRINT
480        GOTO 290
490 REMARK: SET LIABILITIES & CAPITAL TO POSITIVE
500        LET B = B * (-1)
510 REMARK: DETERMINE IF ACCOUNT IS CAPITAL
520        IF A >= 300 GOTO 610
530 REMARK: TOTAL AND PRINT LIABILITIES
540        LET L1 = L1 + B
550        PRINT USING 5, N$, B
560        GOTO 290
570 REMARK: PRINT TOTAL LIABILITIES
580        PRINT USING 6, 'TOTAL LIABLITIES', L1
590        PRINT
600        GOTO 290
610 REMARK: TOTAL AND PRINT CAPITAL
620        LET C1 = C1 + B
630        PRINT USING 5, N$, B
640        GOTO  290
650 REMARK: PRINT NET INCOME, ADD TO CAPITAL AND PRINT TOTAL CAPITAL
660        PRINT USING 5, 'NET INCOME', N1
670        LET C1 = C1 + N1
680        PRINT USING 6, 'TOTAL CAPITAL', C1
690        GOTO 290
700 REMARK: CALCULATE AND PRINT TOTAL LIABILITIES AND CAPITAL
710        LET T1 = L1 + C1
720        PRINT
730        PRINT 'TOTAL LIABILITIES'
740        PRINT USING 6,' AND CAPITAL',T1
750        PRINT USING 7
770 END
```

TOTAL PROGRAM LINES   74

APPENDIX D

AGEREPT

ACCOUNTS RECEIVEABLE SYSTEM

```
  1 REMARK: PRINT IMAGES FOR AGED ACCT.REC. REPORT
  2:################# AGED ACCOUNTS RECEIVABLE REPORT #################
  3 :CUSTOMER     INVOICE     1-30    31-60    61-90   OVER 90
  4 :NO. NAME   NUMBER DATE   DAYS     DAYS     DAYS     DAYS    TOTAL
  5 :### ###############             
  6 :             ####  ##/##  ####.##
  7 :             ####  ##/##          ####.##
  8 :             ####  ##/##                   ####.##
  9 :             ####  ##/##                            ####.##
 10: TOTALS              ####.## ####.## ####.## ####.## ####.##
100 REMARK: INPUT ACCT.REC. MASTER FILE NAME, COMPANY NAME, DATE
110        PRINT 'ENTER ACCT.REC. MASTER FILE NAME';
120        INPUT M$
130        PRINT 'ENTER COMPANY NAME, REPORT DATE';
140        INPUT T$, Y$
150 REMARK: ENTER AGING DATES
160        PRINT 'ENTER MONTH NUMBERS FOR AGING';
170        INPUT D1, D2, D3
180 REMARK: ATTACH ACCT.REC. FILE TO PROGRAM
190        OPEN 1, M$, INPUT
200 REMARK: PRINT REPORT HEADINGS
210        PRINT
220        PRINT USING 2, T$, Y$
230        PRINT
240        PRINT USING 3
250        PRINT USING 4
260        PRINT
270 REMARK: GET CUSTOMER NUMBER, NAME, NUMBER OF INVOICES FROM FILE
280        GET 1: C, N$, X
290        IF C = 999 GOTO 690
300 REMARK: PRINT CUSTOMER NUMBER, NAME
310        PRINT
320        PRINT USING 5, C, N$
330 REMARK: READ INVOICES FOR CUSTOMER
340        IF X = 0 GOTO 600
350        LET L = 0
360        GET 1: I, M, D, A
370 REMARK: DETERMINE AGE CATEGORY TO PRINT INVOICE
380        IF M = D1 GOTO 420
390        IF M = D2 GOTO 460
400        IF M = D3 GOTO 500
410        GOTO 540
420 REMARK: PRINT AND TOTAL 1-30 DAY INVOICES
430        PRINT USING 6, I, M, D, A
440        LET T1 = T1 + A
450        GOTO 570
460 REMARK: PRINT AND TOTAL 31-60 DAY INVOICES
470        PRINT USING 7, I, M, D, A
480        LET T2 = T2 + A
490        GOTO 570
500 REMARK: PRINT AND TOTAL 61-90 DAY INVOICES
510        PRINT USING 8, I, M, D, A
520        LET T3 = T3 + A
530        GOTO 570
540 REMARK: PRINT AND TOTAL ALL INVOICES OLDER THAN 90 DAYS
550        PRINT USING 9, I, M, D, A
560        LET T4 = T4 + A
570 REMARK: DETERMINE IF ALL INVOICES FOR CUSTOMER HAVE PRINTED
580        LET L = L + 1
590        IF L < X GOTO 360
600 REMARK: PRINT CUSTOMER TOTALS AND ADD TO ACCT.REC.LEDGER TOTALS
610        LET T = T1 + T2 + T3 + T4
620        PRINT USING 10, T1, T2, T3, T4, T
630        LET B1 = B1 + T1
640        LET B2 = B2 + T2
```

ACCOUNTS RECEIVEABLE SYSTEM

```
650        LET B3 = B3 + T3
660        LET B4 = B4 + T4
670        LFT T1, T2, T3, T4, L = 0
671 IF C?150 THEN 280
672 FOR Q=1 TO 15
673 PRINT
674 NEXT Q
675 PAUSE
680        GOTO 280
690 REMARK: PRINT ACCT.REC.LEDGER TOTALS
700        LET B = B1 + B2 + B3 + B4
710        PRINT
720        PRINT USING 10, B1, B2, B3, B4, B
740 END
```

TOTAL PROGRAM LINES   79

APPENDIX E

PAY

PAYROLL SYSTEM

```
1 REMARK:  SPECIFY THE PRINT FORMATS
2: ##::::::::::::::::::::::  PAYROLL REGISTER   PERIOD ENDING ##########::::::::
3: EMPLOYEE                WORK HOURS   GROSS          DEDUCTIONS      NET
4:NO.  NAME                REG   OVT    PAY        FIT      FICA      PAY
5:##  #::::::::::::::::::  ##.# ##.#   ####.##   ###.##  ####.##   ####.##
6:        YTD TOTALS ->                          ####.##   ###.##  #####.##  ####.##
7: WEEKLY TOTALS                                ####.##   ###.##  ####.##  ####.##
8        DIM M$(30), D(30), R(30), W(30), Y(30), V(30)
9        DIM X(30), F(30), G(30), P(30), N(30), H(30), S(30)
100 REMARK:  FILE NAMES & PAYROLL DATE INPUT
105      PRINT 'ENTER COMPANY NAME ';
106      INPUT A$
110      PRINT 'ENTER THE PAYROLL CLOSING DATE ';
120      INPUT D$
130      PRINT 'ENTER PAYROLL MASTER FILE NAME AND HOURS FILE NAME';
140      INPUT F$,T$
150 REMARK:  THE FOLLOWING LINKS THE TWO FILES TO THE PROGRAM
160      OPEN 1, F$, INPUT
170      OPEN 3,T$,INPUT
180 REMARK:  MASTER FILE READ ROUTINE
190      GET 1: E
200      IF E = 0 GOTO 250
210      GET 1: M$(E), D(E), R(E), W(E), Y(E), V(E)
220      LET C = E
230      IF C < 30 GOTO 190
240 REMARK:  CURRENT WEEK'S HOURS FILE READ ROUTINE
250      GET 3: E
260      IF E = 0 GOTO 290
270      GET 3: H(E)
280      GOTO 250
285      REMARK:  E WILL BE 0 WHEN IT PASSES THIS POINT
290 REMARK:   CALCULATION ROUTINE
295    REMARK: DETERMINE NO. OF REGULAR & OVERTIME HOURS
300      LET E = E + 1
310      IF H(E) <= 40 GOTO 340
320      LET P(E) = H(E) - 40
330      LET H(E) = 40
```

166

PAYROLL SYSTEM

```
340     REMARK:   GROSS PAY = ( REGULAR PAY )   +  (   OVERTIME PAY   )
350               LET G(E) = ( H(E) * R(E) )  +  ( P(E) * 1.5 * R(E) )
360     REMARK:   STORE YTD GROSS PAY FROM PREVIOUS PERIOD
370        LET L = W(E)
380        LET W(E) = W(E) + G(E)
390     REMARK: CALCULATION OF FEDERAL INCOME TAX DEDUCTION
400        IF 13 * D(E) >= G(E) GOTO 430
410        LET F(E) = .18 * ( G(E)-.13 * D(E) )
420        LET Y(E) = Y(E) + F(E)
430     REMARK:   CALCULATE FICA (SOCIAL SECURITY) DEDUCTION
440        IF L >= 10800   GOTO 510
450        IF W(E) > 10800 GOTO 480
460        LET S(E) = 0.0585 * G(E)
470        GOTO 500
480        LET Q2 = W(E) - 10800
490        LET S(E) = 0.0585 * ( G(E) - Q2 )
500        LET V(E) = V(E) + S(E)
510     REMARK:   COMPUTE NET (TAKE HOME) PAY
520        LET N(E) = G(E) - ( F(E) + S(E) )
530        LET X(E) = W(E) - ( Y(E) + V(E) )
541     REMARK:   SUM PAYROLL TOTALS
542        LET C1 = C1 + G(E)
543        LET C2 = C2 + F(E)
544        LET C3 = C3 + S(E)
545        LET C4 = C4 + N(E)
546        LET C5 = C5 + W(E)
547        LET C6 = C6 + Y(E)
548        LET C7 = C7 + V(E)
549        LET C8 = C8 + X(E)
550        IF E < C GOTO 300
555 REMARK: PRINTING OF RESULTS
560        REMARK:   SET   E=1   TO BEGIN ROUTINE WITH FIRST MAN
570        LET E = 1
580        PRINT
590        PRINT USING 2 , A$ , D$
600        PRINT
610        PRINT USING 3
620        PRINT USING 4
630        PRINT
640        IF G(E) = 0   GOTO 680
650        PRINT USING 5 , E, M$(E), H(E), P(E), G(E), F(E), S(E), N(E)
660        PRINT USING 6 ,                    W(E), Y(E), V(E), X(E)
670        PRINT
680        LET E = E + 1
690        IF E <= C  GOTO 640
695        PRINT USING 7 ,                    C1 ,  C2 ,  C3 ,  C4
697        PRINT USING 6 ,                    C5 ,  C6 ,  C7 ,  C8
700 REMARK: MASTER FILE UPDATE ROUTINE
710        LET E = 1
720        PRINT
730        PRINT'DO YOU WISH TO UPDATE YOUR MASTER FILE (' F$ ') NOW ';
740        INPUT A$
750        IF A$ = 'NO'   GOTO 830
760        IF A$ <>'YES'   GOTO 720
770        OPEN 2, F$,OUTPUT
780        PUT 2:  E, M$(E), D(E), R(E), W(E), Y(E), V(E)
790        LET E = E + 1
800        IF E <= C GOTO 780
810        REMARK:   PUT 2: 0   IS THE END OF FILE INDICATOR
820        PUT 2: 0
830 END
```

TOTAL PROGRAM LINES   100

STLINE

DEPRECIATION METHODS

```
100 REMARK:  SPECIFY THE PRINT FORMATS
110:STRAIGHT LINE DEPRECIATION SCHEDULE FOR ################
120:          BOOK VALUE     ANNUAL              ACCUMULATED     BOOK VALUE
130:YEAR      BEG. OF YR.    DEPRECIATION        DEPRECIATION    END OF YR.
140: ##       #########.##   #########.##        #########.##    #######.##
150 REMARK:  INPUT COST OF ASSET (A), SALVAGE VALUE (S),,
160 REMARK:  AND NUMBER OF YEARS (Y)
170       PRINT 'STRAIGHT LINE DEPRECIATION METHOD'
180       PRINT
190       PRINT 'ENTER COST OF ASSET ';
200       INPUT A
210       PRINT 'ENTER SALVAGE VALUE ';
220       INPUT S
230       PRINT 'ENTER NO. OF YEARS  ';
240       INPUT Y
250 REMARK:  NO. OF MONTHS IN FIRST YEAR (M),
260 REMARK:  AND THE NAME OF THE ASSET (N$).
270       PRINT 'IN FIRST YEAR'
280       PRINT 'ENTER NO. OF MONTHS ';
290       INPUT M
300       PRINT 'ENTER NAME OF ASSET (LESS THAN 16 CHARACTERS) ';
310       INPUT N$
320 REMARK:  PRINTING OF HEADING
330       PRINT
340       PRINT
350       PRINT
360       PRINT USING 110, N$
370       PRINT
380       PRINT USING 120
390       PRINT USING 130
400       PRINT
410 REMARK:  SET BEGINNING BOOK VALUE EQUAL TO COST OF ASSET.
420       B = A
430 REMARK:  VARIABLE (C) IS USED AS A COUNTER FOR THE NUMBER OF YEARS
440       C = C + 1
450 REMARK:  (DEPRECIATION) = (COST OF ASSET - SALVAGE VALUE) / (YEARS)
460       LET   D     =    ( A      -      S )    /  ( Y )
470 REMARK:  TEST FOR PARTIAL FIRST YEAR
480 REMARK:  CONTROL TRANSFERRED TO 550 IF FIRST YR. IS PARTIAL.
490       IF M <> 12 THEN 550
500 REMARK:  CONTROL TRANSFERRED TO 550 IF NO. OF YRS. <= FINAL YR.
510       IF C <= Y THEN 550
520 REMARK:  CONTROL TRANSFERRED TO END IF PROGRAM IS COMPLETE.
530       GO TO 800
540 REMARK:  (Y1) EQUALS THE FINAL YR. IF 1ST. YR. IS PARTIAL.
550       Y1 = Y + 1
560 REMARK:  IF SCHEDULE IS NOT FINISHED THEN CONTROL IS TRANS. TO 610.
570       IF C <= Y1 THEN 610
580 REMARK:  CONTROL IS TRANSFERRED TO END IF SCHEDULE IS COMPLETE.
590       GO TO 800
600 REMARK:  IF THE COUNTER <> 1ST. YR. THEN CONTROL IS TRANS. TO 660.
610       IF C <> 1 THEN 660
620 REMARK:  CALCULATION OF PARTIAL FIRST YEAR DEPRECIATION
630 REMARK:  ( 1 ST. YR. DEP. ) = ( NO. OF MTHS. / 12 ) * ( YRLY DEP. )
640       LET   D     = (   M     / 12.) * (   D    )
650 REMARK:  IF COUNTER <> FINAL YR. THEN CONTROL IS TRANS. TO 730.
660       IF C <> Y1 THEN 720
670 REMARK:  CALCULATION OF PARTIAL LAST YR. DEPRECIATION
680 REMARK:  ( DEP. ) = ( 1 - ( MTHS. / 12. ) ) * ( YRLY DEP. )
690       LET   D   = ( 1 - (  M   / 12. ) ) * (  D   )
700 REMARK:  CALCULATION OF YRLY ENDING BOOK VALUE
710 REMARK:  ( END BOOK VAL ) = ( BEG BOOK VALUE ) - ( DEPRECIATION )
720       LET    B1     = (     B       ) - (    D    )
730 REMARK:  ( ACCUMULATED DEP. ) = ( OLD ACCUM. DEP. ) + ( DEP. )
740       LET    T      = (     T      ) + ( D  )
```

DEPRECIATION METHODS

```
750 REMARK:  PRINTING OF TABLE
760        PRINT USING 140, C, B, D, T, B1
770 REMARK:  END BOOK VAL OF PREVIOUS YR BECOMES BEG BOOK VAL OF NEW YR
780        B = B1
790        GO TO 440
800        END
```

TOTAL PROGRAM LINES   71

APPENDIX G

DEPRECIATION METHODS

```
100 REMARK:  SPECIFY THE PRINT FORMATS
110:SUM OF THE DIGITS (YEARS) DEPRECIATION SCHEDULE FOR ################
120:        BOOK VALUE      ANNUAL        ACCUMULATED     BOOK VALUE
130:YEAR    BEG. OF YR.     DEPRECIATION  DEPRECIATION    END OF YR.
140: ##     ###.###.##      #####.###.##  #########.##    ######.##
150 REMARK:  INPUT COST OF ASSET (A), SALVAGE VALUE (S),
160 REMARK:  AND NUMBER OF YEARS (Y)
170        PRINT 'SUM OF THE DIGITS (YEARS) DEPRECIATION METHOD'
180        PRINT
190        PRINT 'ENTER COST OF ASSET ';
200        INPUT A
210        PRINT 'ENTER SALVAGE VALUE ';
220        INPUT S
230        PRINT 'ENTER NO. OF YEARS  ';
240        INPUT Y
250 REMARK:  INPUT NAME OF THE ASSET
260        PRINT 'ENTER NAME OF ASSET (LESS THAN 16 CHARACTERS) ';
270        INPUT N$
280 REMARK:  PRINTING OF HEADING
290        PRINT
300        PRINT
310        PRINT
320        PRINT USING 110, N$
330        PRINT
340        PRINT USING 120
350        PRINT USING 130
360        PRINT
370 REMARK:  BEG BOOK VALUE = ( COST OF ASSET )
380        LET      B        = (      A        )
390 REMARK:  CALCULATION OF THE SUM OF THE DIGITS (YEARS)
400 REMARK:  IF Z = NUMBER OF YRS. THEN CONTROL IS TRANSFERRED TO 470
410        IF      Z =       Y        THEN      470
420 REMARK:  VARIABLE ( Z ) IS A COUNTER FOR THE YEARS
430        LET Z = Z + 1.
440 REMARK:  VARIABLE ( X ) IS A SUMMER FOR THE SUM OF THE YRS DIGITS
450        LET X = X + Z
460        GO TO 390
470 REMARK:  VARIABLE (C) IS USED AS A COUNTER FOR THE NUMBER OF YEARS
480        LET C = C + 1
490 REMARK:  CALCULATION OF THE YRLY DEPRECIATION RATE
500 REMARK:  RATE = ( YEARS - ( PRESENT YR - 1. ) ) / (SUM OF YRS)
510        LET R = (   Y   - (   C   - 1. ) ) / (   X   )
520 REMARK:  CALCULATION OF THE YRLY DEPRECIATION
530 REMARK:  DEPRECIATION = (RATE) * (ASSET - SALVAGE VALUE)
540        LET      D        = ( R ) * ( A   -       S        )
```

169

DEPRECIATION METHODS

```
550 REMARK:  CALCULATION OF YRLY ENDING BOOK VALUE
560 REMARK:  ( ENDING BOOK VAL ) = ( BEG BOOK VAL ) - ( DEPRECIATION )
570     LET        B1      = (      B      ) - (      D      )
580 REMARK:  CALCULATION OF YRLY ACCUMULATED DEPRECIATION
590 REMARK:  ( ACCUMULATED DEP. ) = ( OLD ACCUM. DEP. ) + ( DEP. )
600     LET        T       = (      T      ) + (  D  )
610 REMARK:  PRINTING OF TABLE
620     PRINT USING 140 , C , B , D , T , B1
630 REMARK:  END BOOK VAL OF PREVIOUS YR BECOMES BEG BOOK BAL OF NEW YR
640     LET B = B1
650 REMARK:  IF THE YRS COMPLETED < FINAL YR THEN CONTROL GOES TO 480
660     IF C < Y THEN 480
680     END
```

TOTAL PROGRAM LINES   58

APPENDIX H

DECLINE

DEPRECIATION METHODS

```
100 REMARK:  SPECIFY THE PRINT FORMATS
110:DECLINING BALANCE DEPRECIATION SCHEDULE FOR ##############
120:        BOOK VALUE      ANNUAL          ACCUMULATED      BOOK VALUE
130:YEAR   BEG. OF YR.   DEPRECIATION     DEPRECIATION     END OF YR.
140: ##    ########.##   ########.##     ########.##      #######.##
150 REMARK:  INPUT COST OF ASSET (A), SALVAGE VALUE (S),,
160 REMARK:  AND NUMBER OF YEARS (Y)
170     PRINT 'DECLINING BALANCE DEPRECIATION METHOD'
180     PRINT
190     PRINT 'ENTER COST OF ASSET ';
200     INPUT A
210     PRINT 'ENTER SALVAGE VALUE ';
220     INPUT S
230     PRINT 'ENTER NO. OF YEARS  ';
240     INPUT Y
250 REMARK:  INPUT DECLINING BALANCE DEPRECIATION RATE.
260     PRINT 'ENTER DEPRECIATION RATE IN PERCENT';
270     INPUT P
280 REMARK:  NO. OF MONTHS IN FIRST YEAR (M),
290 REMARK:  AND THE NAME OF THE ASSET (N$).
300     PRINT 'IN FIRST YEAR'
310     PRINT 'ENTER NO. OF MONTHS ';
320     INPUT M
330     PRINT 'ENTER NAME OF ASSET (LESS THAN 16 CHARACTERS) ';
340     INPUT N$
350 REMARK:  PRINTING OF HEADING
360     PRINT
370     PRINT
380     PRINT
390     PRINT USING 110, N$
400     PRINT
410     PRINT USING 120
420     PRINT USING 130
430     PRINT
440 REMARK:  SET BEGINNING BOOK VALUE EQUAL TO COST OF ASSET.
450     B = A
500 REMARK: RATE = ST LINE RATE * PERCENTAGE
510     LET R = ( 1/Y )    * ( P/100 )
```

170

DEPRECIATION METHODS

```
520 REMARK:  VARIABLE (C) IS USED AS A COUNTER FOR THE NUMBER OF YRS.
530       C = C + 1
540 REMARK:  CALCULATE YEARLY DEPRECIATION.
550 REMARK:  ( DEPRECIATION ) = ( RATE ) * ( BOOK VALUE )
560       LET      D      = ( R  ) * (    B    )
570 REMARK:  TEST FOR PARTIAL FIRST YEAR.
590       IF M <> 12 THEN 650
600 REMARK:  CONTROL TRANSFERRED TO 710 IF NO. OF YRS. <= FINAL YR.
610       IF C <=  Y THEN 710
630       GO TO 990
640 REMARK:  (Y1) EQUALS THE FINAL YR. IF 1ST. YR. IS PARTIAL.
650       Y1 = Y + 1
660 REMARK:  IF SCHEDULE IS NOT FINISHED THEN CONTROL IS TRANS. TO 710.
670       IF C <= Y1 THEN 710
690       GO TO 990
700 REMARK:  IF THE COUNTER <> 1ST. YR. THEN CONTROL IS TRANS. TO 760.
710       IF C <> 1 THEN 760
720 REMARK:  CALCULATION OF PARTIAL FIRST YEAR DEPRECIATION
730 REMARK:  ( 1 ST. YR. DEP. ) = ( NO. OF MTHS. / 12 ) * ( YRLY DEP . )
740       LET      D      = (    M      / 12.) * (      D      )
750 REMARK:  IF COUNTER <> FINAL YR. THEN CONTROL IS TRANS. TO 820.
760       IF C <> Y1 THEN 820
770 REMARK:  CALCULATION OF PARTIAL LAST YR. DEPRECIATION
780 REMARK:  ( DEP. ) = ( 1 - ( MTHS. / 12. ) ) * ( YRLY DEP. )
790       LET   D   = ( 1 - (  M   / 12. ) ) * (    D    )
800 REMARK:  CALCULATION OF YRLY ENDING BOOK VALUE
810 REMARK:  ( ENDING BOOK VAL. ) = ( BEG. BK. VAL. ) - ( DEPRECIATION )
820       LET      B1      = (    B      ) - (    D      )
850  REMARK:   IF SAL. VAL. < END. BAL. THEN CONTROL IS TRANS. TO 920
860       IF S < B1 THEN 920
870 REMARK:  CALCULATION OF DEP. WHEN YRLY DEP. >= END. BOOK VALUE.
880 REMARK:  ( DEPRECIATION ) = ( BEG. BOOK VALUE ) - ( SALVAGE VALUE )
890       LET      D      = (    B      ) - (    S    )
900 REMARK:  ( ENDING BOOK VALUE ) = ( SALVAGE VALUE )
910       LET      B1      = (    S    )
920 REMARK:  PRINTING OF TABLE
922 REMARK:  ( ACCUMULATED DEP. ) = ( OLD ACCUM. DEP. ) + ( DEP. )
924       LET      T      = (      T      ) + ( D  )
930       PRINT USING 140, C, B, D, T, B1
940 REMARK:  END BOOK VAL OF PREVIOUS YR BECOMES BEG BOOK VAL OF NEW YR
950       B = B1
960 REMARK:  IF SAL. VAL. < ENDING BK VAL THEN CONTROL IS TRAN TO 520
970       IF S < B1 THEN 520
990       END
```

TOTAL PROGRAM LINES   82

APPENDIX I

UNITS

DEPRECIATION METHODS

```
100       DIM U(50)
110 REMARK:  SPECIFY THE PRINT FORMATS
120:UNITS OF PRODUCTION DEPRECIATION SCHEDULE FOR ##########'::.##
130:        BOOK VALUE      ANNUAL                        BOOK VALUE
140:YEAR    BEG. OF YR.     DEPRECIATION      UNITS       END OF YR.
150: ##     ##########.##   ##########.## ##### OF #####  #######.##
160 REMARK:  INPUT COST OF ASSET (A), SALVAGE VALUE (S).,
```

DEPRECIATION METHODS

```
170 REMARK:  AND NUMBER OF YEARS (Y)
180       PRINT 'UNITS OF PRODUCTION METHOD'
190       PRINT
200       PRINT 'ENTER COST OF ASSET ';
210       INPUT A
220       PRINT 'ENTER SALVAGE VALUE ';
230       INPUT S
240       PRINT 'ENTER NO. OF YEARS  ';
250       INPUT Y
255       PRINT 'ENTER ESTIMATED UNITS OF PRODUCTION'
260 REMARK:  VARIABLE C IS A COUNTER FOR YEARS
270       LET C = C + 1
280 REMARK:  ENTER ESTIMATED UNIT PRODUCTION FOR EACH YEAR
300       PRINT 'FOR YR. NUMBER'C;
310       INPUT U(C)
320 REMARK:  VARIABLE X IS A SUMMER FOR ESTIMATED TOTAL UNITS PRODUCED
330       LET X = X + U(C)
340 REMARK:  IF # OF YRS < FINAL YR THEN CONTROL IS TRANSFERRED TO 270
350       IF C < Y THEN 270
360 REMARK:  VARIABLE C IS SET TO ZERO
370       LET C = 0
380       PRINT 'ENTER NAME OF ASSET (LESS THAN 16 CHARACTERS) ';
390       INPUT N$
400 REMARK:  PRINTING OF HEADING
410       PRINT
420       PRINT
430       PRINT USING 120, N$
440       PRINT
450       PRINT USING 130
460       PRINT USING 140
470       PRINT
480 REMARK:  SET BEGINNING BOOK VALUE EQUAL TO COST OF ASSET.
490       B = A
500 REMARK:  CALCULATION OF DEPRECIATION RATE PER UNIT
510 REMARK:  RATE = ( ASSET - SALVAGE VALUE ) / ( TOTAL UNITS )
520       LET R   = (    A    -       S      ) / (    X      )
530 REMARK:  VARIABLE (C) IS USED AS A COUNTER FOR THE NUMBER OF YEARS
540       C = C + 1
550 REMARK:  CALCULATION OF YRLY DEPRECIATION
560 REMARK:  DEPRECIATION = ( RATE ) * ( EST. YRLY PRODUCTION )
570       LET    D      = (  R  ) * (        U(C)           )
580 REMARK:  CALCULATION OF YRLY ENDING BOOK VALUE
590 REMARK:  ( END BOOK VAL ) = ( BEG BOOK VALUE ) - ( DEPRECIATION )
600       LET     B1      = (      B       ) - (     D     )
610 REMARK:  ( ACCUMULATED DEP. ) = ( OLD ACCUM. DEP. ) + ( DEP. )
620       LET       T        = (       T        ) + (  D  )
630 REMARK:  PRINTING OF TABLE
640       PRINT USING 150, C, B, D, U(C), X, B1
650 REMARK:  END BOOK VAL OF PREVIOUS YR BECOMES BEG BOOK VAL OF NEW YR
660       B = B1
670 REMARK:  IF COUNTER < FINAL YR THEN CONTROL IS TRANSFERRED TO 540
680       IF     C    <     Y  THEN  540
690 END
```

TOTAL PROGRAM LINES   60

APPENDIX J

BEGBAL

GENERAL LEDGER ORIGIN FILE

100	100,	CASH	,	7000.00
110	120,	ACCTS.RECEIVABLE	,	8000.00
120	150,	COMPUTER EQUIP.	,	9000.00
130	155,	DEPRECIATION	,	-1000.00
140	170,	PROGRAM COPYRIGHTS	,	15000.00
150	1,	ASSETS	,	0.00
160	200,	ACCTS.PAYABLE	,	-4500.00
170	220,	NOTES PAYABLE	,	-12000.00
180	230,	TAXES PAYABLE	,	-3000.00
190	2,	LIABILITIES	,	0.00
200	300,	W S WILSON CAPITAL	,	-13200.00
210	3,	CAPITAL	,	0.00
220	400,	FEES EARNED	,	-40000.00
230	4,	INCOME	,	0.00
240	500,	SALARIES	,	16000.00
250	510,	BAD DEBT EXPENSE	,	200.00
260	520,	COMPUTER EXPENSE	,	14000.00
270	530,	DEPR. EXPENSE	,	0.00
280	540,	OFFICE SUPPLIES	,	2000.00
290	550,	TRAVEL & ENTERTAIN	,	2000.00
300	560,	UTILITIES	,	500.00
310	5,	EXPENSE	,	0.00
999	999,	END	,	0.00

APPENDIX K

GLCREATE

GENERAL LEDGER SYSTEM

```
100 REMARK: PROGRAM TO INITIALIZE STUDENT GENERAL LEDGER FILE
110    REMARK: SPECIFY THE NAMES OF THE ORIGIN & MASTER FILES
120       PRINT 'ENTER NAME OF YOUR GENERAL LEDGER ORIGIN FILE    ';
130       INPUT B$
140       OPEN 1, B$, INPUT
150       PRINT 'ENTER NAME OF YOUR GENERAL LEDGER MASTER FILE    ';
160       INPUT G$
170       OPEN 2, G$, OUTPUT
180    REMARK: READ CHART OF ACCOUNTS AND STORE ON STUDENT FILE
190       GET 1: A, N$, B
200       PUT 2: A, N$, B
210    REMARK: ACCOUNT NUMBER 999 SIGNALS END OF FILE
220       IF A = 999 GOTO 260
230    REMARK: TOTAL ACCOUNT BALANCES
240       LET T = T + B
250       GOTO 190
260    REMARK: PRINT TRIAL BALANCE OF INITIAL FILE
270       PRINT
280       PRINT USING 290, T
290       :YOUR GENERAL LEDGER BEGINNING TRIAL BALANCE IS #####.##
310 END
```

TOTAL PROGRAM LINES   21

GLEDIT

GENERAL LEDGER SYSTEM

```
100 REMARK: GENERAL LEDGER TRANSACTIONS EDIT PROGRAM
110     DIM A(50),N$(50),B(50)
120   REMARK: SPECIFY FILE NAMES
130     PRINT 'ENTER THE NAME OF YOUR GENERAL LEDGER FILE';
140     INPUT G$
150     PRINT 'ENTER THE NAME OF YOUR TRANSACTION FILE   ';
160     INPUT T$
170   REMARK: READ VALID ACCOUNT NUMBER FROM MASTER FILE
180     OPEN 1, G$, INPUT
190     LET I = 1
200     GET 1: A(I), N$(I), B(I)
210     IF A(I) = 999 GOTO 240
220     LET I = I + 1
230     GOTO 200
240   REMARK: READ A SOURCE TRANSACTION
250     OPEN 2, T$, INPUT
260     GET 2: E, D$, R, V
270     IF E = 999 GOTO 400
280   REMARK: CHECK FOR VALID ACCOUNT NUMBER ON TRANSACTION
290     LET K = 1
300     IF E = A(K) GOTO 350
310     LET K = K + 1
320     IF K < I GOTO 300
330     PRINT 'ACCOUNT';E;'IS INVALID. THE TRANSACTION WILL NOT BE POSTED.'
340     GOTO 260
350   REMARK: TOTAL AMOUNTS OF ALL ACCEPTED TRANSACTIONS
360     LET T = T + V
370   REMARK: COUNT NUMBER OF TRANSACTIONS ACCEPTED
380     LET C = C + 1
390     GOTO 260
400   REMARK: PRINT TOTAL OF ALL ACCEPTED TRANSACTIONS
410     PRINT
420     PRINT C; 'TRANSACTIONS ACCEPTED'
430     PRINT USING 440, T
440     :TOTAL OF ALL TRANSACTIONS ACCEPTED IS   #####.##
460 END
```

TOTAL PROGRAM LINES   36

ARBEGIN

ACCOUNTS RECEIVEABLE ORIGIN FILE

```
100    100,    CAFE PARIS         ,   3
110    1065,   5,    15,      75.75
120    1101,   6,    20,     100.05
130    1122,   7,     5,      75.95
140    110,    DRAKE HOTEL        ,   3
150    1059,   4,    29,      50.00
160    1087,   6,    10,     100.00
170    1120,   7,     1,     150.50
180    120,    FIRST STATE BANK   ,   2
```

ACCOUNTS RECEIVEABLE ORIGIN FILE

```
190    1107,    6,    25,       75.00
200    1133,    7,    15,       24.75
210    130,     HENRY JONES              ,    2
220    1062,    5,    10,       75.25
230    1085,    6,     6,       50.00
240    140,     KINGS HOTEL              ,    4
250    1066,    5,    15,      100.00
260    1080,    6,     5,       75.35
270    1112,    6,    25,      100.95
280    1130,    7,    15,      125.00
290    150,     JANICE LONG              ,    1
300    1135,    7,    15,      150.00
310    160,     LONDON GRILL             ,    0
320    170,     MRS.M.PETERSON           ,    6
330    1052,    4,    15,       55.00
340    1071,    5,    15,       75.25
350    1082,    6,     5,      125.00
360    1102,    6,    20,       35.00
370    1125,    7,    12,      125.35
380    1136,    7,    15,       90.00
390    180,     RUSTY COMPANY            ,    3
400    1079,    5,    25,       25.35
410    1095,    6,    15,       75.00
420    1134,    7,    15,      100.00
430    190,     STATEWIDE AIRLINES  ,    2
440    1105,    6,    25,      100.00
450    1131,    7,    15,      205.75
460    200,     WILLIAM TUCKER           ,    1
470    1137,    7,    15,       75.75
480    210,     J.W.WASHINGTON           ,    1
490    1096,    6,    15,       25.00
500    220,     WILSON COMPANY           ,    3
510    1100,    6,    15,       60.60
520    1123,    7,     7,      120.00
530    1138,    7,    27,       70.25
999    999,     END                      ,    0
```

APPENDIX N

ARCREATE

ACCOUNTS RECEIVEABLE SYSTEM

```
100 REMARK: PROGRAM CREATES STUDENT ACCOUNTS RECEIVABLE MASTER FILE
110     PRINT'ENTER NAME OF YOUR ACCT.REC. ORIGIN FILE ';
120     INPUT F$
130     PRINT'ENTER NAME OF YOUR ACCT.REC. MASTER FILE ';
140     INPUT M$
150 REMARK: ATTACH FILES TO PROGRAM
160     OPEN 1,F$,INPUT
170     OPEN 2,M$,OUTPUT
180 REMARK: READ DATA FROM CASE PROBLEM FILE TO STUDENT FILE
190     GET 1: C, N$, X
200     PUT 2: C, N$, X
210     IF C = 999 GOTO 340
220 REMARK: COUNT NUMBER OF CUSTOMERS ON FILE
230     LET T = T + 1
240 REMARK: READ AND STORE EACH INVOICE FOR CUSTOMER
250     IF X = 0 GOTO 190
260     GET 1: I, M, D, A
270     PUT 2: I, M, D, A
```

175

ACCOUNTS RECEIVEABLE SYSTEM

```
280     REMARK: TOTAL AMOUNT OF ALL INVOICES
290        LET T1 = T1 + A
300        LET L = L + 1
310        IF L < X GOTO 260
320        LET L = 0
330        GOTO 190
340     REMARK: PRINT CONTROL TOTALS
350        PRINT
360        PRINT USING 370, T1
370        :ACCOUNTS RECEIVABLE LEDGER TOTALS TO ######.##
380        PRINT T;'CUSTOMERS ON ACCOUNTS RECEIVABLE FILE'
400 END
```

TOTAL PROGRAM LINES   30

APPENDIX O

ARPOST

ACCOUNTS RECEIVEABLE SYSTEM

```
  1 REMARK: SPECIFY PRINT IMAGES FOR CONTROL TOTALS
  2 :TOTAL OF PAYMENTS POSTED            = ######.##
  3 :TOTAL OF NEW INVOICES POSTED        = ######.##
  4 :TOTAL OF ACCOUNTS RECEIVABLE LEDGER FILE = ######.##
100 REMARK: INPUT MASTER FILE NAME, TRANSACTION FILE NAME
110        PRINT 'ENTER ACCT.REC. MASTER FILE NAME, TRANSACTION FILE NAME';
120        INPUT M$, T$
130        DIM C(50), N$(50), X(50), I(50, 48)
140 REMARK: READ MASTER FILE
150        OPEN 1, M$, INPUT
160        LET J = 1
170     REMARK: READ CUSTOMER NUMBER, NAME, NUMBER OF INVOICES
180        GET 1: C(J), N$(J), X(J)
190        IF C(J) = 999 GOTO 320
200     REMARK: READ ALL INVOICES FOR A CUSTOMER
210        IF X(J) = 0 GOTO 300
220        LET L = 0
230        LET K = 1
240        GET 1: I(J,K), I(J,K+1), I(J,K+2), I(J,K+3)
250        LET T3=T3+I(J,K+3)
260        LET L = L + 1
270        IF L = X(J) GOTO 300
280        LET K = K + 4
290        GOTO 240
300        LET J = J + 1
310        GOTO 180
320 REMARK: ATTACH TRANSACTION FILE TO PROGRAM
330        OPEN 2, T$, INPUT
340 REMARK: READ TRANSACTION FROM TRANSACTION FILE
350        GET 2: C1, I1, M, D, A
360        IF C1 = 999 GOTO 810
370 REMARK: SEARCH MASTER FILE FOR TRANSACTION CUSTOMER NUMBER
380        LET J = 1
390        IF C(J) = C1 GOTO 450
400        LET J = J + 1
410        IF C(J) <> 999 GOTO 390
420 REMARK: REJECT TRANSACTION WHEN CUSTOMER NUMBER NOT ON MASTER FILE
430        PRINT 'CUST.';C1;'NOT ON MASTER FILE--TRANSACTION REJECTED'
440        GOTO 340
```

ACCOUNTS RECEIVEABLE SYSTEM

```
450 REMARK: DETERMINE IF TRANSACTION IS A NEW INVOICE OR A PAYMENT
460        IF A < 0 GOTO 600
470 REMARK: INSERT NEW INVOICE INTO 1ST UNUSED POSITION
480        LET K = 1
490        IF I(J,K) = 0 GOTO 520
500        LET K = K + 4
510        GOTO 490
520        LET I(J,K) = I1
530        LET I(J,K+1) = M
540        LET I(J,K+2) = D
550        LET I(J,K+3) = A
560        LET X(J) = X(J) + 1
570 REMARK: TOTAL NEW INVOICES ENTERED
580        LET T1 = T1 + A
590        GOTO 340
600 REMARK: SEARCH CUSTOMER RECORD FOR PAYMENT INVOICE
610        LET L = 0
620        LET K = 1
630        IF I(J,K) = 0 GOTO 670
640        IF I(J,K) = I1 GOTO 720
650        LET L = L + 1
660        IF L = X(J) GOTO 690
670        LET K = K + 4
680        GOTO 630
690 REMARK: REJECT PAYMENT TRANSACTION WHEN INVOICE NOT ON FILE
700        PRINT 'INV.';I1;'FOR CUST.';C1;'NOT ON MASTER FILE--TRANS REJECTED'
710        GOTO 340
720 REMARK: SUBTRACT PAYMENT AMOUNT FROM INVOICE
730        LET I(J,K+3) = I(J,K+3) + A
740 REMARK: WHEN INVOICE PAID IN FULL, DELETE IT FROM RECORD
750        IF I(J,K+3) <> 0 GOTO 780
760        LET I(J,K), I(J,K+1), I(J,K+2), I(J,K+3) = 0
770        LET X(J) = X(J) - 1
780 REMARK: TOTAL ALL PAYMENT TRANSACTIONS
790        LET T2 = T2 + A
800        GOTO 340
810 REMARK: AT END OF POSTING, PRINT CONTROL TOTALS
820        PRINT
830        PRINT USING 2, T2
840        PRINT USING 3, T1
850        PRINT USING 4,T3+T1+T2
860 REMARK: DETERMINE IF UPDATED ACCT.REC. RECORDS ARE TO BE STORED
870        PRINT
880        PRINT 'DO YOU WISH TO UPDATE YOUR ACCT.REC. MASTER FILE NOW ';
890        INPUT Y$
900        IF Y$ = 'NO' GOTO 1070
910 REMARK: STORE UPDATED ACCT.REC. RECORDS
920        OPEN 1, M$, OUTPUT
930        LET J = 1
940        PUT 1: C(J), N$(J), X(J)
950        IF C(J) = 999 GOTO 1080
960        IF X(J) = 0 GOTO 1050
970        LET L = 0
980        LET K = 1
990        IF I(J,K) = 0 GOTO 1030
1000       PUT 1: I(J,K), I(J,K+1), I(J,K+2), I(J,K+3)
1010       LET L = L + 1
1020       IF L = X(J) GOTO 1050
1030       LET K = K + 4
1040       GOTO 990
1050       LET J = J + 1
1060       GOTO 940
1080 END
```

ARCHANGE

ACCOUNTS RECEIVEABLE SYSTEM

```
  1 REMARK: PRINT IMAGES FOR CONTROL TOTALS FOR CHANGES TO ACCT.REC.FILE
  2:TOTAL OF WRITE-OFF OF UNCOLLECTABEL INVOICES = #####.##
100 REMARK: ENTER ACCT.REC. MASTER FILE NAME
110        PRINT 'ENTER ACCT.REC. MASTER FILE NAME';
120        INPUT M$
130 REMARK: READ MASTER FILE
140        OPEN 1, M$, INPUT
150        DIM C(50), N$(50), X(50), I(50,36)
160        LET J = 1
170        GET 1: C(J), N$(J), X(J)
180        IF C(J) = 999 GOTO 290
190        IF X(J) = 0 GOTO 270
200        LET L = 0
210        LET K = 1
220        GET 1: I(J,K), I(J,K+1), I(J,K+2), I(J,K+3)
230        LET L = L + 1
240        IF L = X(J) GOTO 270
250        LET K = K + 4
260        GOTO 220
270        LET J = J + 1
280        GOTO 170
290        LET J9 = J
300 REMARK: ENTER TYPE OF CHANGE
310        PRINT
320        PRINT 'ENTER CODE FOR TYPE OF CHANGE:'
330        PRINT '1=WRITE-OFFS; 2=NEW CUSTOMER; 3=DELETE CUSTOMER; 4=END'
340        INPUT C9
350 REMARK: BRANCH TO SELECTED CHANGE ROUTINE
360        GOTO 390, 660, 760, 900 ON C9
370        PRINT 'CODE INVALID..RE-ENTER';
380        GOTO 340
390 REMARK: WRITE-OFF UNCOLLECTABLE INVOICES
400        PRINT 'ENTER CUSTOMER, INVOICE FOR WRITE-OFF';
410        INPUT C1, I1
420 REMARK: SEARCH FOR CUSTOMER RECORD
430        LET J = 1
440        IF C(J) = C1 GOTO 490
450        LET J = J + 1
460        IF J < J9 GOTO 440
470        PRINT 'CUSTOMER';C1;'NOT ON ACCT.REC.MASTER FILE'
480        GOTO 300
490 REMARK: SEARCH FOR INVOICE TO WRITE-OFF
500        LET L = 0
510        LET K = 1
520        IF X(J) = 0 GOTO 590
530        IF I(J,K) = 0 GOTO 570
540        IF I(J,K) = I1 GOTO 610
550        LET L = L + 1
560        IF L = X(J) GOTO 590
570        LET K = K + 4
580        GOTO 530
590        PRINT 'INVOICE';I1;'NOT ON FILE FOR CUSTOMER';C1
600        GOTO 300
610 REMARK: DELETE INVOICE FROM CUSTOMER RECORD AND TOTAL WRITE-OFFS
620        LET T1 = T1 + I(J,K+3)
630        LET I(J,K), I(J,K+1), I(J,K+2), I(J,K+3) = 0
640        LET X(J) = X(J) - 1
650        GOTO 300
660 REMARK: ADD NEW CUSTOMER TO FILE
670        PRINT 'ENTER CUSTOMER NUMBER, CUSTOMER NAME';
680        INPUT C1, N$
690 REMARK: ADD NEW CUSTOMERS TO END OF FILE
700        LET C(J9) = C1
710        LET N$(J9) = N$
```

178

ACCOUNTS RECEIVEABLE SYSTEM

```
720        LET X(J9) = 0
730        LET J9 = J9 + 1
740        LET T2 = T2 + 1
750        GOTO 300
760 REMARK: DELETE CUSTOMERS FROM THE FILE
770        PRINT 'ENTER CUSTOMER NUMBER';
780        INPUT C1
790 REMARK: SEARCH FOR CUSTOMER
800        LET J = 1
810        IF C(J) = C1 GOTO 860
820        LET J = J + 1
830        IF J < J9 GOTO 810
840        PRINT 'CUSTOMER NOT ON ACCT.REC. FILE'
850        GOTO 300
860 REMARK: SET CUSTOMER NUMBER TO ZERO
870        LET C(J) = 0
880        LET T3 = T3 + 1
890        GOTO 300
900 REMARK: STORE UPDATED MASTER FILE
910        OPEN 1,M$,OUTPUT
920        LET J = 1
930        IF C(J) = 0 GOTO 950
940        PUT 1: C(J), N$(J), X(J)
950        IF X(J) = 0 GOTO 1050
960        LET L = 0
970        LET K = 1
980        IF I(J,K) = 0 GOTO 1030
990        IF C(J) = 0 GOTO 1010
1000       PUT 1: I(J,K), I(J,K+1), I(J,K+2), I(J,K+3)
1010       LET L = L + 1
1020       IF L = X(J) GOTO 1050
1030       LET K = K + 4
1040       GOTO 980
1050       LET J = J + 1
1060       IF J < J9 GOTO 930
1070 REMARK: PUT END OF FILE RECORD
1080       PUT 1: 999,'END',0
1100 REMARK: PRINT CONTROL TOTALS
1110       PRINT
1120       PRINT USING 2,T1
1130       PRINT T2;'NEW CUSTOMERS ADDED TO MASTER FILE'
1140       PRINT T3;'CUSTOMERS DELETED FROM MASTER FILE'
1150 END
```

TOTAL PROGRAM LINES   107

APPENDIX Q

CREATE

PAYROLL SYSTEM

```
100 PRINT 'ENTER THE NAME OF YOUR PAYROLL ORIGIN FILE ';
110 INPUT P$
120 PRINT'ENTER THE NAME OF YOUR PAYROLL MASTER FILE ';
130 INPUT O$
140 OPEN 1, P$, INPUT
150 OPEN 2, O$, OUTPUT
160 GET 1: A
170 IF A=0 GOTO 250
```

CREATE

PAYROLL SYSTEM

```
180 GET 1:    B$,C,D,E,F,G
210 PUT 2: A,B$,C,D,E,F,G
220 LET X = X+1
230 IF X=9 GOTO 250
240 GOTO 160
250 PRINT
260 PRINT X;'PAYROLL MASTER RECORDS PUT IN FILE    : ';O$
270 PUT 2: 0
280 END
```

TOTAL PROGRAM LINES   17

APPENDIX R

PAY1

PAYROLL ORIGIN FILE

```
100  1, HENRY WILLIAMS, 2,  3.75 ,   6125.00 , 1092.10 , 358.31
110  2, DONALD COOLEY , 1,  4.50 ,   8188.00 , 1468.64 , 479.00
120  3, RAYMOND HARRIS, 4,  3.25 ,   6080.00 , 1073.60 , 355.68
130  4, VINCENT HUMM  , 3,  3.50 ,   5250.00 ,  929.40 , 307.12
140  5, CARTER ZAPCO  , 2,  2.50 ,   4764.00 ,  847.12 , 278.69
150  6, FRANK KESTER  , 5,  5.25 , 10750.00 , 1909.00 , 628.87
160  7, PHYLLIS GISH  , 1,  3.10 ,   4920.00 ,  880.40 , 287.82
170  0
```

APPENDIX S

ADJUST

PAYROLL SYSTEM

```
   1 REMARK: PRINT FORMATS
   2:                                    < - - - YEAR TO DATE TOTALS - - - >
   3: EMPLOYEE                TAX   PAY    GROSS      DEDUCTIONS         NET
   4:NO.  NAME               DED   RATE    PAY      FIT     FICA        PAY
   5:##  ##############-####  ##  ###.##  #####.##  #####.##  #####.##  #####.##
   6:(1)   (2)               (3)  (4)      (5)       (6)      (7)       (8)
1000        PRINT 'ENTER PAYROLL MASTER FILE NAME ';
1010        INPUT F$
1020        OPEN 1, F$, INPUT
1030 REMARK:  MASTER FILE READ ROUTINE
1035        LET C = 0
1040        GET 1: E
1050        IF E = 0 GOTO 1090
1060        GET 1:  M$(E), D(E), R(E), W(E), Y(E), V(E)
1070        LET C = C + 1
1080        IF C < 30 GOTO 1040
1090 REMARK:  SELECT ROUTINE DESIRED
```

PAYROLL SYSTEM

```
1100        PRINT'USE FUNCTION CODE 88 FOR INSTRUCTIONS !'
1110        PRINT
1120        PRINT'FUNCTION DESIRED ( 0 TO END )  '!
1130        INPUT O
1140        GOTO  1420,1520,1700,1960,1210 ON O
1150        IF O = 88 GOTO 1830
1160        IF O = 0  GOTO 2350
1170        PRINT'VALID FUNCTIONS ARE 1,2,3,4 OR 5 '
1180        PRINT'RE-ENTER YOUR FUNCTION NO. '!
1190        GOTO 1130
1210 REMARK:  UPDATE THE MASTER FILE
1220        OPEN 2, F$,OUTPUT
1230        LET E = 1
1240        PUT 2:  E, M$(E), D(E), R(E), W(E), Y(E), V(E)
1250        LET E = E + 1
1260        IF E <= C GOTO  1240
1270        REMARK:  PUT 2: 0  IS THE END OF FILE INDICATOR
1280        PUT 2: 0
1290        GOTO 2390
1300 REMARK:  PRINT ROUTINE
1310        IF P = 1 GOTO 1390
1320        PRINT
1330        PRINT USING 2
1340        PRINT USING 3
1350        PRINT USING 4
1360        PRINT USING 6
1370        PRINT
1380        LET P = 1
1390        LET N = W(E) - ( Y(E) + V(E) )
1400        PRINT USING 5, E, M$(E), D(E), R(E), W(E), Y(E), V(E), N
1410        RETURN
1420 REMARK: LIST THE FILE ROUTINE
1430        LET P = 0
1440        PRINT
1450        FOR E = 1 TO C
1470        GOSUB 1300
1480        NEXT E
1490        PRINT
1500        PRINT
1510        GOTO 1120
1520 REMARK:  ADD A RECORD ROUTINE
1530        PRINT
1540        PRINT USING 1550, C + 1
1550        :THE NEW EMPLOYEE'S NUMBER IS ##
1560        PRINT'ENTER  EMPLOYEE NAME, TAX DED., HOURLY PAY RATE '
1570        PRINT'       ( EG.   JOHN SMITH , 2 , 3.75 )'
1580        LET E = C + 1
1590        INPUT M$(E), D(E),R(E)
1600        PRINT
1610        GOSUB 1300
1620        PRINT
1630        PRINT'IS ABOVE OK '!
1640        INPUT Z$
1650        IF Z$ =  'NO'  GOTO 1560
1660        IF Z$ <> 'YES' GOTO 1630
1670        LET C = C + 1
1680        PRINT
1690        GOTO 1120
1700 REMARK:  DELETE RECORD FROM ACTIVE STATUS
1710        PRINT
1720        PRINT'DELETE EMPLOYEE NO. '!
1730        INPUT E
1740        PRINT
1750        GOSUB 1300
1760        PRINT
1770        PRINT'IS THIS THE RIGHT EMPLOYEE '!
1780        INPUT Z$
1790        IF Z$ =  'NO'  GOTO 1710
1800        IF Z$ <> 'YES' GOTO 1760
1810        LET R(E) = 0
1820        GOTO 1110
```

181

PAYROLL SYSTEM

```
1830 REMARK: PRINT OUT INSTRUCTIONS OF THE FUNCTIONS AVAILABLE
1840        PRINT
1850        PRINT'FUNCTIONS AVAILABLE ARE:'
1860        PRINT
1870        PRINT'      1   LIST THE RECORDS IN THE FILE'
1880        PRINT'      2   ADD A NEW EMPLOYEE RECORD '
1890        PRINT'      3   DELETE AN EMPLOYEE RECORD '
1900        PRINT'          FROM ACTIVE (PAY) STATUS.'
1910        PRINT'      4   MAKE CHANGES TO A RECORD.'
1920        PRINT'      5   UPDATE THE MASTER FILE ('F$') WITH THE CHANGES'
1930        PRINT
1940        PRINT
1950        GOTO 1010
1960 REMARK:  CHANGE INDIVIDUAL ITEMS IN  A RECORD
1970        PRINT
1980        PRINT'EMPLOYEE NO. ';
1990        INPUT E
2000        PRINT
2010        GOSUB 1300
2020        PRINT
2030        PRINT'IS THIS THE RIGHT EMPLOYEE ';
2040        INPUT Z$
2050        IF Z$ =  'NO'  GOTO 1970
2060        IF Z$ <> 'YES' GOTO 2020
2070        PRINT
2080        PRINT'WHICH COLUMN (FIELD) TO BE CHANGED (2 THRU 7)
2090        PRINT'  ( 0 = NO MORE CHANGES )          ';
2100        INPUT F
2110        PRINT
2120        IF F <> 0 GOTO 2150
2130        GOSUB 1300
2140        GOTO 1110
2150        GOTO 2070,2170,2200,2230,2260,2290,2340 ON F
2160        GOTO 2070
2170        PRINT 'ENTER CORRECT NAME  ';
2180        INPUT M$(E)
2190        GOTO 2070
2200        PRINT'ENTER NO. OF TAX DEDUCTIONS ';
2210        INPUT D(E)
2220        GOTO 2070
2230        PRINT'ENTER NEW PAY RATE ';
2240        INPUT R(E)
2250        GOTO 2070
2260        PRINT'ENTER CORRECT YEAR-TO-DATE GROSS PAY ';
2270        INPUT W(E)
2280        GOTO 2070
2290        PRINT'ENTER CORRECT YEAR-TO-DATE FIT DEDUCTIONS ';
2300        INPUT Y(E)
2310        GOTO 2070
2320        PRINT'ENTER CORRECT YEAR-TO-DATE FICA DEDUCTIONS ';
2330        INPUT V(E)
2340        GOTO 2070
2350 REMARK:  STOP WITHOUT UPDATING THE MASTER FILE
2360        PRINT
2370        PRINT'RUN TERMINATED...MASTER FILE NOT UPDATED.'
2380        GOTO 2400
2390        PRINT'THE MASTER FILE ('F$') IS UPDATED.'
2400 END
```

TOTAL PROGRAM LINES   146

HOURS

PAYROLL SYSTEM

```
  1 REMARK: CREATES INDIVIDUAL WEEKLY HOURS FILES
100 REMARK: READ VALID EMPLOYEE NUMBERS FROM MASTER FILE
110       PRINT 'ENTER THE NAME OF YOUR MASTER PAYROLL FILE';
120       INPUT F$
130       OPEN 1,F$,INPUT
140       DIM M(30)
150       GET 1: E
160       IF E = 0 GOTO 210
170       GET 1: M$, D, R, W, Y, V
180       IF R = 0 GOTO 150
190       M(E) = E
200       GOTO 150
210 REMARK: SPECIFY HOURS FILE NAME
220       PRINT 'ENTER THE NAME OF YOUR HOURS FILE   ';
230       INPUT T$
240       OPEN 2,T$,OUTPUT
250       PRINT
260       PRINT 'ENTER EMPLOYEE NUMBER, HOURS (0,0 TO END) '
270       INPUT E,H
275 IF E>30 GOTO 310
280       IF E = 0 GOTO 390
290   REMARK: EDIT EMPLOYEE NUMBER AS VALID
300       IF M(E) = E GOTO 330
310       PRINT 'INVALID EMPLOYEE NUMBER. RE-ENTER'
320       GOTO 270
330 REMARK: PUT ON HOURS FILE EMPLOYEE NUMBER AND HOURS WORKED
340       PUT 2: E, H
350 REMARK: TOTAL NUMBER OF EMPLOYEES AND TOTAL OF THEIR HOURS
360       LET C = C + 1
370       LET T = T + H
380       GOTO 270
390 REMARK: PRINT CONTROL TOTALS
400       PRINT
410       PRINT C ; 'EMPLOYEE HOURS ENTRIES PUT ON THE FILE  : ';T$
420       PRINT T ; 'TOTAL HOURS ENTERED.'
430       PUT 2:0
440 END
```

TOTAL PROGRAM LINES   37

INDEX